KT-592-919

The AA POCKETGuide
MADEIRA

Madeira: Regions and Best places to see

Original text by Christopher Catling

Updated by Christopher Catling

© Automobile Association Developments Limited 2008

First published 2008

ISBN: 978-0-7495-5521-4

Published by AA Publishing, a trading name of Automobile Association Developments Limited, whose registered office is Fanum House, Basing View, Basingstoke, Hampshire RG21 4EA. Registered number 1878835.

Colour separation: Keenes, Andover

Printed and bound in Italy by Printer Trento S.r.l.

Front cover images: (t) AA/C Sawyer; (b) AA/J Wyand

Back cover image: AA/J Wyand

A03404

Maps in this title produced from mapping © KOMPASS GmbH, A-6063 Rum/Innsbruck

About this book

This book is divided into four sections.

Planning pages 6–19
Before You Go; Getting There; Getting Around; Being There

Best places to see pages 20–41
The unmissable highlights of any visit to Madeira

Exploring pages 42–127
The best places to visit in Madeira, organized by area

Maps pages 131–142
All map references are to the atlas section. For example, Calheta has the reference 🟦 132 F3 – indicating the page number and grid square in which it is to be found

Contents

Planning

Before You Go

WHEN TO GO

JAN	FEB	MAR	APR	MAY	JUN	JUL	AUG	SEP	OCT	NOV	DEC
18°C	19°C	19°C	20°C	21°C	22°C	24°C	25°C	25°C	23°C	22°C	19°C
64°F	66°F	66°F	68°F	70°F	72°F	75°F	77°F	77°F	73°F	72°F	66°F

High season   Low season

The temperatures given in the above table are the daily average for each month. Madeira is warm even during the winter, and not too hot in summer. From July to September it can be humid, and it might get too chilly to eat outside at night during November to April, though nights can be just as warm as the days from May to October.

Madeira's weather varies according to the time of day, geography or altitude. For example, it could be very sunny in the morning, raining in the afternoon and then clear in the evening. The southern part of the island tends to have more sun. Between 800 and 1,000m (2,600 and 3,300ft) rain clouds occur, but above these altitudes it is generally clear.

WHAT YOU NEED

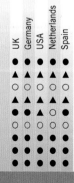

		UK	Germany	USA	Netherlands	Spain
● Required	Some countries require a passport to remain valid					
○ Suggested	for a minimum period (usually at least six months)					
▲ Not required	beyond the date of entry – contact their consulate or embassy or your travel agent for details.					
Passport (or National Identity Card where applicable)		●	●	●	●	●
Visa (regulations can change – check before you travel)		▲	▲	▲	▲	▲
Onward or Return Ticket		○	○	○	○	○
Health Inoculations (tetanus and polio)		▲	▲	▲	▲	▲
Health Documentation (►9, Health Advice)		●	●	▲	○	●
Travel Insurance		○	○	○	○	○
Driving Licence (national)		●	●	●	●	●
Car Insurance Certificate		●	●	●	●	●
Car Registration Document		●	●	●	●	●

ADVANCE PLANNING
WEBSITES
www.madeiratourism.org
www.madeiraonline.com
www.madeira-island.com
www.madeira-live.com
www.madeiraguide.com
www.madeira-web.com

TOURIST OFFICES AT HOME
In the UK
Portuguese National Tourist Office
22–25A Sackville Street,
London W1S 3EJ
☎ 020 7494 5720

In the USA
Portuguese National Tourist Office
590 Fifth Avenue, 4th Floor,
New York, NY 10036–4704
☎ 800/767 8842

HEALTH ADVICE
Insurance
Nationals of EU countries can receive free emergency medical treatment on Madeira on production of the relevant documentation (a European Health Insurance Card), although private medical insurance is still advised and is essential for all other visitors. You can apply for an EHIC at the Post Office, online at **www.**dh.gov.uk/travellers or by calling the EHIC Application Line (☎ 0845 606 2030).

Dental services
Dental services on Madeira are generally excellent. Dentists advertise their services in the free English- and German-language magazines that are available from most hotels and the tourist information centre in Funchal.

TIME DIFFERENCES

GMT 12 noon	Portugal 12 noon	Germany 1PM	USA (NY) 7AM	Netherlands 1PM	Spain 1PM

Madeira, like mainland Portugal, observes Greenwich Mean Time (GMT) during the winter months; during the summer, from late March to late September, the time is GMT plus 1 hour.

WHAT'S ON WHEN

January *Grand New Year Firework Show* (starts midnight 31 Dec): the New Year starts with a bang and noisy blowing of ships' hooters at one of Europe's most spectacular public fireworks festivals.

Dia de Reis (6 Jan): the Day of the Kings, with its religious services and special cakes, marks the end of Christmas and the New Year celebrations.

February *Carnival* (four days before Ash Wednesday): *Carnival* is celebrated all over Madeira, but the costumed parades in Funchal are definitely the best. On the Saturday before Ash Wednesday the highly professional Grand Carnival Parade takes place, when large themed floats, complete with live bands and up to 150 dancers, form a festive spectacle. On Shrove Tuesday itself, the Public Parade is a chance for local clubs and groups to dress up and compete for prizes.

April *Flower Festival* (second or third weekend): Funchal becomes a blaze of colour for this festival, when shops, houses and churches are all decorated with ribbons and flags, and children make a wall of flowers in Praça do Município. The climax is a parade through Funchal with bands and colourful floats.

June *Fins de Semana Musicais* (all month) Musical Weekends: Madeira's music festival features guest musicians and talented students from the local conservatoire performing in the cathedral and Teatro Baltazar Dias.

August *Feast of the Assumption* (15 Aug): Madeira's biggest religious festival is celebrated with church services by day and dancing, fireworks and feasting by night. Penitents visit the church at Monte to climb the steps on their knees.

September *Madeira Wine Festival* (early Sep): in Funchal and Câmara de Lobos, the completion of the wine harvest is celebrated with public demonstrations of wine-treading, local music and dance and wine tastings.

NATIONAL HOLIDAYS

JAN	FEB	MAR	APR	MAY	JUN	JUL	AUG	SEP	OCT	NOV	DEC
1	1	(1)	2	1	2	1	2		1	1	4

1 Jan	New Year's Day
Feb (dates vary)	Shrove Tuesday and Ash Wednesday
Mar/Apr	Good Friday, Easter Monday
25 Apr	Day of the Revolution
1 May	Labour Day
Jun (date varies)	Corpus Christi
10 Jun	National Day
1 Jul	Madeira Day
15 Aug	Feast of the Assumption
21 Aug	Funchal Day
5 Oct	Republic Day
1 Nov	All Saints' Day
1 Dec	Restoration of Independence Day
8 Dec	Immaculate Conception
25/26 Dec	Christmas

Most shops, offices and museums close on these days.

October *Festa da Maçã* (25–26 Oct): the Apple Festival in Camacha offers an opportunity to sample the apples grown around the village, and to enjoy local folk singing and dancing, made more enjoyable by glasses of cider and apple brandy.

November *Festa da Castanha* (1 Nov): the chestnut harvest in Curral das Freiras provides an excuse to consume chestnuts in many forms.

December *Christmas Illuminations* (from 8 Dec): the build-up to Christmas begins when the street illuminations are officially switched on by a local dignitary.

Christmas Cribs (from 16 Dec): the Portuguese tradition of building tableaux representing the crib continues in Funchal, and in many villages.

Village festivals
Village festivals celebrate the feast day of the local saint, to whom the parish church is dedicated, or some special event in the history of the village (such as the procession in Machico on 8 October in honour of the crucifix that survived the destruction of the local church).

Getting There

BY AIR

Cruise ships regularly call at
Funchal on the way to the
Caribbean, but most visitors to
Madeira arrive by air. Santa Catarina
(Funchal) airport is served by flights
from most European airports, either
direct or via Lisbon. TAP Air Portugal
is the national airline (in Funchal
☎ 213 141).

The airport is 22km (13.5 miles)
from the centre of Funchal. Most

visitors are met by tour
respresentatives on arrival and
their onward transport is generally
prearranged. As a result demand for
public transport is not great and
independent visitors may have no
choice but to take a taxi to the
centre of Funchal (around 35
minutes). The alternative is the
airport bus, which departs at
roughly 90-minute intervals and
takes around 50 minutes.

Getting Around

DRIVING

Drive on the right.

Speed limit on motorways: **110kph (68mph)**
Speed limit on main roads: **80kph (50mph)**
Speed limit on urban roads: **60 or 40kph (37 or 25mph)**

It is mandatory for drivers and passengers to wear seat belts if fitted.

Random breath-testing takes place. Never drive under the influence of alcohol.

Petrol (gasolina) comes in two grades: lead-free (sem chumbo) and lead-substitute (super). Diesel (gasóleo) is also available. Most villages and towns have a petrol station, and they are generally open from 8 to 8. The GALP petrol station on Avenida do Infante, in Funchal, is open 24 hours. Most take credit cards.

Because all visitors to Madeira drive rental cars, there is no central breakdown and rescue service. Instead, the car rental companies operate their own breakdown services, with repairs usually being carried out promptly. The documents you are given on renting the car will explain what to do in the event of a breakdown.

PUBLIC TRANSPORT

INTERNAL FLIGHTS

There are several flights a day from Funchal to Porto Santo. The 37km (23-mile) journey takes 15 minutes, and flights are heavily booked in high season, so be sure to reserve well in advance. Flights can be reserved through any travel agent or through branches of TAP Air

Portugal. On Madeira TAP's office is at Avenida das Comunidades Madeirenses 10 (☎ 213 141).

BUSES

A highly efficient bus system connects all towns with Funchal. Buses are modern and comfortable (though they do not have safety belts) and most drivers take care to drive safely on Madeira's tortuous roads.

Buses within Funchal and its suburbs are painted orange; those serving the rural areas are operated by five different companies, each with its own livery. Nearly all buses depart from the bus stops along Avenida do Mar, where you can also buy tickets from the bus company kiosks (7-day go-as-you-please passes are available to visitors only, so bring your passport if you want to buy one). Up-to-date timetables can be bought from the tourist office on Avenida Arriaga.

BOAT TRIPS

The old ferry service has been replaced by a sleek new cruise ship that promises smoother sailings and many onboard facilities; the journey time is 2 hours 40 minutes. Tickets can be bought in advance from travel agents, or from the office of the Porto Santo Line, Rua da Praia 6, Funchal (☎ 210 300).

Several cruise companies operate out of Funchal's yachting marina, all offering half- or full-day excursions around Madeira's coastline. Turipesca (☎ 231 063) operates charter cruises, game-fishing trips and regular cruises (including evening cruises with dinner).

TAXIS

There are taxi ranks in towns and taxis may also stop if flagged down, especially in the countryside. Rates for out-of-town journeys (eg from Funchal to the airport) are fixed. Short journeys are metered. For longer journeys, you can negotiate an hourly or half-day rate.

CAR RENTAL

The major car rental firms are represented on Madeira, as well as several local companies, which offer competitive rates. You can reserve a car in advance through travel agents, at the airport on arrival or through your hotel. All rental firms will deliver your car to you.

CONCESSIONS

Students/youths Museums and attractions have lower rates of admission for students and for children aged 4 to 14 (under-4s are free). Bring a passport or student card as proof of your age.

Senior citizens Many senior citizens come to Madeira for the winter months, attracted by warm weather, a low cost of living and heavily discounted low-season long-stay rates. Ask travel agents specializing in Madeira for details.

Being There

TOURIST OFFICES

Funchal Avenida Arriaga 18
☎ 211 902

Machico Forte de Nossa Senhora
do Amparo ☎ 962 289

Porto Santo Avenida Henrique
Vieira de Castro ☎ 983 562

Ribeira Brava Forte de Sâo Bento
☎ 951 675

Santana Sítio do Serrado
☎ 572 992

Some travel agencies in Funchal advertise themselves as if they were tourist information centres, though their primary aim is to sell you one of their organized tours. In general these tours (by mini bus or coach) are good value and the standards of safety are high. You must expect, however, that the tour will include time spent in shops and restaurants rather than sightseeing – you may prefer to have the flexibility of your own taxi with driver, which can work out as cheap as an organized tour if three or four people share a car.

CONSULATES
UK ☎ 221 221
Germany ☎ 220 338
USA ☎ 235 636
Netherlands ☎ 703 803

TELEPHONES
Telephones are found in cafés and on streets in larger towns. Some only take phonecards, available from newsagents and cafés. To call Madeira or Porto Santo from abroad dial 00 351 (the international code for Portugal) then 291 (the area code for both islands). In Madeira and Porto Santo you only need to dial the subscriber number.

OPENING HOURS

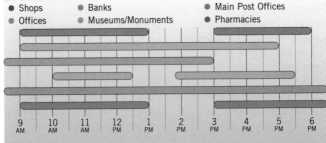

- Shops
- Offices
- Banks
- Museums/Monuments
- Main Post Offices
- Pharmacies

| 9 AM | 10 AM | 11 AM | 12 PM | 1 PM | 2 PM | 3 PM | 4 PM | 5 PM | 6 PM |

Small shops are open Monday to Saturday 9 or 10am to 7 or 8pm. Some close early on Saturday and only those aimed at tourist open on Sunday. Larger stores and supermarkets are open continuously from 10 to 10, seven days a week. Pharmacies open late on a duty rota (posted on pharmacy doors). Village post offices have shorter opening hours; main post offices also open Saturday morning.

INTERNATIONAL DIALLING CODES

From Madeira (Portugal) to:
UK 00 44
Germany 00 49
USA and Canada 00 1
Netherlands 00 31
Spain 00 34

EMERGENCY TELEPHONE NUMBERS

Police 112
Fire 112
Ambulance 112

POSTAL SERVICES

Post offices (Correios) are found in the main towns. In Funchal, the most central post office is on Avenida do Zarco. Poste restante services are available at the main post office on Rua Dr Joao Brito Camara. Stamps can also be bought from many newsagents. Open: Mon–Fri 8.30–8, Sat 9–12.30.

ELECTRICITY

The power supply on Madeira is: 220 volts AC. Sockets accept continental two-pronged plugs, so an adaptor is needed for non-continental appliances, and a transformer for devices operating on 100–120 volts.

CURRENCY AND EXCHANGE

Currency Portugal's currency is the euro (€), divided into 100 cents. Coins come in denominations of 1, 2, 5, 10, 20 and 50 cents and 1 and 2 euros. Notes come in denominations of 5, 10, 20, 50, 100 and 500 euros (the last two are rarely seen).

MasterCard, Visa, American Express and Diners cards are widely accepted, as are travellers' cheques.

Exchange Banks with exchange bureaux are found in Funchal and the larger towns. Commission on changing euro travellers' cheques can be high.

HEALTH AND SAFETY

Sun advice The sun can be intense on Madeira at any time of the year, and it is possible to burn with less than an hour's exposure. If you are out walking on bare mountains, it is best to cover vulnerable parts of your body, including your neck, legs and arms.

Drugs Chemists *(farmâcia)* are open Mon–Fri 9–1 and 3–7, and Sat 9–12.30. Some open through the lunch break, and there is a late-night duty rota, posted in pharmacy windows. Take supplies of any drugs that you take regularly, since there is no guarantee that they will be available locally.

TIPS/GRATUITIES

	Yes ✓ No ✗	
Restaurants (service and tax included)	✓	10%
Bar service	✓	change
Taxis	✓	10%
Porters	✓	€1.50
Chambermaids	✗	
Swimming pool attendants	✗	
Hairdressers	✓	10%
Tour guides	✓	€5
Toilets	✗	

Safe water Tap water is safe to drink everywhere. It is fresh and often comes straight from pure mountain springs. Mineral water is available everywhere; if you ask for fizzy water (*água com gás*), rather than still (*água sem gás*), it is likely to be naturally sparkling, rather than carbonated.

Crime Incidents are extremely rare, but in the unlikely event that you are the victim of theft, report your loss to the main police station at the Rua Dr João de Deus 7 (☎ 222 022) and get a copy of the written statement in order to support your insurance claim.
- Leave your valuables in the hotel.
- Do not leave valuables in cars.
- Do not leave unattended valuables on the beach or poolside.
- Beware of pickpockets in markets and on crowded streets.

PHOTOGRAPHY

What to photograph: Madeira's mountainous landscape will provide you with many subjects, including waterfalls, sheer cliffs, volcanic landscapes and deep ravines. For colour, there are markets, flowers and traditional costumes.

Best time to photograph: the light is best before 10am, after which you can expect haze and clouds. Sunsets are brief but colourful.

CLOTHING SIZES

France	UK	Rest of Europe	USA	
46	36	46	36	
48	38	48	38	
50	40	50	40	
52	42	52	42	
54	44	54	44	**Suits**
56	46	56	46	
41	7	41	8	
42	7.5	42	8.5	
43	8.5	43	9.5	
44	9.5	44	10.5	
45	10.5	45	11.5	**Shoes**
46	11	46	12	
37	14.5	37	14.5	
38	15	38	15	
39/40	15.5	39/40	15.5	
41	16	41	16	
42	16.5	42	16.5	**Shirts**
43	17	43	17	
36	8	34	6	
38	10	36	8	
40	12	38	10	
42	14	40	12	
44	16	42	14	**Dresses**
46	18	44	16	
38	4.5	38	6	
38	5	38	6.5	
39	5.5	39	7	
39	6	39	7.5	
40	6.5	40	8	**Shoes**
41	7	41	8.5	

Best places to see

1 Adegas de São Francisco

Visit a wine lodge set in a medieval monastery to sample Madeira and learn how it is produced.

To step from the bustle of Funchal's main street into the calm courtyards of the Adegas de São Francisco is to enter a world where time has a different meaning. Here, on payment of a fairly substantial sum, you can buy wines that were bottled in the 1860s, while upstairs, slowly maturing in huge barrels of Brazilian satinwood and American oak, are wines that nobody living today is likely to taste. As Churchill said, 'to drink Madeira is to sip history with every glass'.

The lodge, with its romantic timber buildings and wisteria-hung balconies, started life as the monastery of St Francis and was converted to its present use in 1834. At that time, Madeira wines were still being sent on board ship to the equator and back in the belief that the rocking motion

improved the wine. The production process was revolutionised by the accidental discovery that Madeira's unique quality comes not from motion but from gentle heating. Now the wine is 'cooked' in vast vats using the warmth of the sun, boosted when necessary by the heat from hot water pipes. All this becomes clear as you tour the cobbled yard to see ancient wooden presses and leather-bound wine ledgers, learn the subtle arts of the wine blender and visit the warming rooms, with their deliciously heady smell of old wood and wine. Scents such as these are a prelude to the pleasures to come as you head for the sampling that concludes this popular tour, which takes place in a room with delightful murals painted in 1922 by Max Römer.

✚ 142 B3 ✉ Avenida Arriaga 28, Funchal ☎ 740 110
🕐 Mon–Fri 9.30–6.30, Sat 10–1. Guided tours: Mon–Fri 10.30, 2.30, 3.30, 4.30, Sat 11. 'Vintage Experience' tours Wed, Fri 4.30. Closed Sun, public hols 👋 Moderate
🍴 Theatre café (€) opposite
🛈 Avenida Arriaga 18

2 Cabo Girão

The towering cliff face of Cabo Girão can be viewed from a boat or from the dizzy heights of its clifftop balcony.

Cabo Girão is not quite Europe's highest sea cliff – it is beaten into second place by a Norwegian competitor – but at 580m (1,902ft) it is impressive enough. Girão means 'turning', an apt description of the vertiginous effect of looking down to the sea from the clifftop. In fact, it is said that the name dates from Zarco's first voyage of discovery when he set out to explore the Madeiran coast in 1420. His diary vividly describes sailing 'towards a dark, stupendous object ... abode of demons and evil spirits'. Deciding to venture no further, Zarco turned back at this point to seek a safe anchorage at what is now the fishing port of Câmara de Lobos (➤ 84–85).

For a different view of Cabo Girão you can retrace Zarco's voyage by taking a boat excursion along Madeira's southern coast. Numerous companies offer tours from Funchal, and you can either book direct by visiting the marina, or through hotels and travel agents. Half-day tours go as far west as Ponta do Sol (➤ 72), and most operators anchor off Cabo Girão so that you can dive off the boat and swim in the clean, warm waters. One company, Turipesca, also offers fishing trips.

Alternatively, you can take a cable car down the face of the cliff to the beach at its base, where brave and hardy farmers cultivate vines on handkerchief-sized plots, taking advantage of the warmth stored in these south-facing rocks.

✚ 137 E6 ✉ 22km (13.5 miles) west of Funchal, and 10km (6 miles) west of Câmara de Lobos 🍴 Snack bar (€) alongside the viewing platform 🚌 Bus 154 from Funchal 🚢 Details of boat excursions from companies based in the yacht marina, such as Turipesca (☎ 231 063) and Costa do Sol (☎ 238 538) ❓ For the cable car take the Fajãs turning off Via Rápida after Câmara de Lobos and follow signs for 'Teleférico' (✉ 944 248)

3 Curral das Freiras

This secret valley, known as the Nuns' Corral (or Refuge), is hidden among the peaks of Madeira's central mountain range.

Only with mild exaggeration did H N Coleridge, nephew of the poet, describe Curral das Freiras (the name literally means Nuns' Refuge) as 'one of the great sights of the world'. The majestic peaks that encircle the village certainly invite such claims, though quiet contemplation of the views can sometimes be difficult because of the sheer number of visitors in high season. If you prefer relative solitude, the best way to find it is to walk into the village along the old zig-zag path that starts at Eira do Serrado, high above the village, parking alongside the newly built café, shop and hotel.

Until 1959, this cobbled path was the only way in and out of the village. Its impregnability was the reason why the nuns of Santa Clara Convent (► 46) fled here in 1566 to escape from piratical raids on Funchal. Even if you don't want to walk all the way down, it is still

worth stopping at Eira do Serrado in order to enjoy the plummeting views from the lookout point (Miradouro) located just a short walk from the hotel. From here, the village far below seems to sit in the bowl of a vast crater, surrounded by sheer cliffs rising to jagged peaks. The view is not quite so enthralling from the bottom looking up, but there are other compensations: bars in Curral das Freiras sell the local speciality, a delicious chestnut-flavoured liqueur called *licor de castanha*, as well as bread, soup and cakes made from chestnuts, all of which are harvested in autumn from trees growing in woods all around the village.

✚ 137 C7 ✉ 20km (12.5 miles) northwest of Funchal 🖐 Free 🍴 Nuns' Valley Restaurant (€) in the centre of the village 🚌 Bus 81 from Funchal

4 Mercado dos Lavradores, Funchal

The covered market in Funchal is a full of colourful island produce, a great place to shop for fruit, flowers and souvenirs.

The Workers' Market was built in 1937 as a producers' market, where island farmers and fishermen could bring their produce for sale direct to the public. Now professional retailers predominate, but the original spirit prevails on Friday, as farmers from the remotest corners of Madeira descend on Funchal in loaded-down pick-up trucks to sell their home-grown produce.

Flower-sellers in traditional island costume have colonised the entrance to the market. Their stalls sell keenly priced cut flowers and bulbs – tubs full of amaryllis bulbs, freshly dug and smelling of earth, or delicate orchid blooms might tempt you to buy a souvenir of the island's horticultural richness.

In the fish hall, there are scenes to turn the stomach. If the razor-sharp teeth and large staring eyes of the scabbard fish do not give you nightmares, the sight of huge tuna fish being gutted and filleted may well.

For pleasanter sights and fragrances, head for the upper floor, with its lavish displays of seasonal fruit and vegetables. If you are self-catering on Madeira, you could do worse than come here to buy good fresh food.

✚ 142 E2 ✉ Rua Dr Fernão Ornelas 🕐 Mon–Thu 7–4, Fri 7–8, Sat 7–5. Closed Sun 🍴 Many stalls selling snacks, plus bars and pavement cafés in the nearby Zona Velha

5 The Monte Toboggan Ride

The quintessential Madeira experience is to slide in a metal-shod toboggan down the steep cobbled streets linking Monte to Funchal.

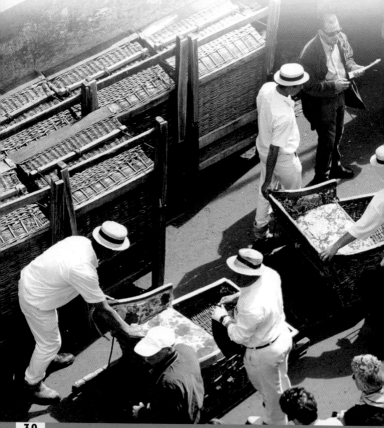

Was Ernest Hemingway being ironic when he described the Monte toboggan ride as one of the most exhilarating experiences of his life? The only way to find out is to try it for yourself by heading up to the hill town of Monte, high above Funchal. Here you can join the line of apprehensive travellers queuing to slide back down to the capital in a wicker basket mounted on polished metal runners. Two toboggan drivers, wearing rubber-soled boots for grip, will push and steer you over the bumpy cobbles and ensure that you do not come to grief as you negotiate sharp bends.

The ride no longer goes all the way to Funchal. Instead, it ends in the suburb of Livramento, some 2km (1.2 miles) downhill. Some visitors consider this brief but unique journey to be the highlight of their visit to Madeira – others consider it overpriced hype (as well as the price of the ride, you will be expected to tip the toboggan drivers, and pay for the souvenir photographs that are taken as you descend and presented to you at the journey's end).

✚ 138 D1 ✉ Toboggan rides start from the foot of the steps of Nossa Senhora do Monte church 🕐 Toboggan rides are available Mon–Sat 9–6, Sun 9–1 ✋ Expensive 🍴 Café (€) frequented by toboggan drivers alongside church steps 🚌 Town bus 20, 21, 22 or Teleféricos da Madeiras (➤ 40)

6 Museu de Arte Sacra, Funchal

Enjoy masterpieces of Flemish art, paid for by Madeira's highly profitable sugar trade with northern Europe.

Funchal's Sacred Art Museum is housed in the former bishop's palace, built in 1600 and given its gracious cobbled courtyard and entrance staircase when the building was remodelled between 1748 and 1757. Displayed on the first floor is a collection of ancient religious vestments, silverware and statuary collected from remote churches all over Madeira. Some of these objects date to the earliest years of the island's colonization, including the intricately decorated processional cross donated to Funchal Cathedral by the Portuguese King Manuel I, who reigned from 1490 to 1520.

The best of the museum's treasures are displayed on the upper floor. Here you can enjoy the naturalism and human pathos of several beautiful painted wooden statues of the Virgin and Child, as well as the warm colours of several fine Flemish masterpieces. For many years it was not

known who painted these remarkable pictures of the Nativity, the Crucifixion and of various saints. By comparison with works by known artists, scholars have now deduced that they are principally the work of leading painters based in Bruges and Antwerp in the late 15th and early 16th centuries, including Gerard David (1468–1523), Dieric Bouts (died 1475) and Jan Provost (1465–1529). Several paintings include portraits of the donors, wealthy merchants who made a fortune from the Madeiran sugar trade. One fine example shows an Italian merchant, Simon Acciaiuoli, kneeling at prayer with his Scottish wife, Mary Drummond, in a painting of the *Descent from the Cross*, while another shows Simon Gonçalves da Câmara, the grandson of Zarco, Madeira's discoverer, and his family.

✚ 142 C2 ✉ Rua do Bispo 21 ☎ 228 900 🕐 Tue–Sat 10–12.30, 2.20–6, Sun 10–1. Closed Mon, public hols 🍴 Café do Museu (€) at rear of museum

7

Palheiro Gardens

The botanical riches of Africa, Asia and the Americas are combined in the beautifully landscaped gardens of this aristocratic estate.

Of all the gardens on Madeira, those surrounding the Quinta do Palheiro Ferreiro (originally known as Blandy's Gardens) are the most rewarding. Here the spirit of the English garden has been transposed to Madeira, where full advantage has been taken of the frost-free environment. Plants that would curl up and die further north, or which have to be cosseted in the hothouse, thrive here out of doors. To create this lovely garden, successive generations of the Blandy family have been able to draw on the limitless treasures of the botanical world, planting gorgeous proteas from southern Africa, flame-flowered climbers from southern America,

sweetly scented Japanese flowering shrubs, and Chinese trees with exotically patterned bark. The result is a garden full of surprises and unexpected plant combinations.

The English influence is evident in the division of the garden into a series of 'rooms' divided by hedges and linked by mixed borders. Smaller intimate areas, such as the peaceful and shady Ladies' Garden, with its topiary peacocks, give way to more open areas, such as the sweeping lawns surrounding the baroque chapel built by the Count of Carvalhal.

The wealthy count was the original owner of this aristocratic estate, which the Blandy family acquired in 1885. Part of the estate remains exactly as the count laid it out in the late 18th century, including the stately avenue of gnarled old plane trees that leads up to his original mansion. Beyond the mansion is an extensive area of informal woodland, signposted 'Inferno' (Hell), where blue morning glory vines trail among primeval tree ferns from New Zealand.

✠ 138 E2 ✉ São Gonçalo, 8km (5 miles) east of Funchal ☎ 793 044 🕐 Mon–Fri 9–4.30. Closed Sat, Sun 🖐 Moderate 🍽 Tea House (€) 🚌 Town bus 36, 37

8 Pico do Arieiro

Drive to the top of Madeira's third highest peak for raw volcanic landscapes and spectacular views, best enjoyed at sunset or sunrise.

Pico do Arieiro (1,818m/ 5,965ft) is the third highest peak on Madeira. It is easily reached from central Funchal by driving north on the EN 103 road to the Poiso Pass, and then taking the EN 202 west.

As you climb, the green woodland that cloaks much of central Madeira gives way to a wilder upland landscape of sheep-grazed turf. The sense of travelling to a different world is reinforced by the cloud belt, which hangs at around 1,200m (3,900ft). Passing through this miasma of swirling mist and driving rain, you will emerge in brilliant sunshine. Bare rock soon becomes the predominant feature in the landscape, and only the hardiest of plants can find any toehold among the clinker-like tufa that makes up the summit of Pico do Arieiro.

To compensate for the lack of vegetation, there are tremendous views over an endless succession of knife-edge ridges and sheer cliffs. Cotton-wool clouds hang in the valleys far below and the only sound comes from the wind. The predominant colours are purple, burnt orange and chocolate brown, a reminder of Madeira's volcanic origins. The rocks are even more vividly colourful when lit by the red and orange rays of the setting sun, or the pink light of dawn.

✚ 134 E3 🍴 Snack bar (€)

Sé (Funchal Cathedral)

Founded in 1485, Funchal's cathedral is one of Madeira's oldest buildings and a link with the island's original settlers.

Portugal's King Manuel I was so proud of his newly acquired island province that, in 1485, he decided to send one of Lisbon's top architects, Pedro Enes, to build a new cathedral for Funchal. The result, completed in 1514, is essentially a sombre building, although it is enlivened with Arabic-style architectural details. The most lavish exterior decoration is found not around the entrance portal, as is customary, but at the east end of the church, where the roofline is decorated with pinnacles shaped like miniature minarets. These echo the

shape of the spire, which is covered in glazed *azulejos* (tiles) that were originally intended to protect the structure from wind and rain, rather than act as decoration. The comparatively plain portal bears King Manuel I's coat of arms at the top, incorporating the red cross of the Knights Templar, of which Manuel was the Grand Master.

The cool interior of the cathedral reveals its secrets only slowly as your eyes adapt to the darkness. High above the nave is a carved wooden ceiling inlaid with geometric designs in ivory. If you look long enough, or use binoculars, you will begin

to make out strange animals and exotic flowers among the designs. Easier to appreciate are the choir stalls, boldly carved with near-lifesize figures of the Apostles, painted in gold against a background of powder blue. The Apostles are dressed in stylish hats, cloaks, tunics, boots and belts, giving us a good idea of the kind of clothes worn by prosperous Madeiran sugar merchants when the stalls were carved in the early 16th century. More entertaining scenes from contemporary life are to be found carved on the undersides of the choir seats. As well as cherubs, you will find monkeys and pigs and a porter carrying a pigskin full of wine.

✚ 142 C2 ✉ Largo da Sé ☎ 228 155 ⏰ Mon–Sat 9–12.30, 4–5.30 (services early morning and early evening) ⑨ Free 🍴 Many pavement cafés (€) on cathedral square

10 Zona Velha (Old Town), Funchal

For atmosphere, inexpensive food and authentic Portuguese *fado* music, Funchal's Zona Velha is the best place to head.

Funchal's Zona Velha (Old Town), formerly the city's slum, is now an area of quaint cobbled streets with craft shops occupying the low, one-roomed houses where at one time whole families slept, ate and played. The former boatyard has been filled in to create the base station for the Teleféricos da Madeiras (Madeira Cable Car), while opposite the station is the Madeira Story Centre (➤ 53, 55), a great place to go at the beginning of your visit to Madeira to gain a sense of the island's history. At the eastern end, under the walls of the Fortaleza de São Tiago (➤ 48), there is a tiny black-pebble beach

(the Praia da Barreirinha) where local people still come to bathe and eat grilled sardines sold by street vendors. The Old Town's last remaining fishermen also repair their boats here.

The beach remains popular despite the new lido, complete with swimming pools and sea-bathing facilities, just beyond the fortress. Opposite the lido stands the Igreja do Socorro (also called Santa Maria Maior), rebuilt several times since it was founded in the 16th century in thanksgiving for the ending of an epidemic. By contrast, the tiny Capela do Corpo Santo, in the heart of the old town, remains a simple 16th-century fishermen's chapel.

Surrounding the chapel are pavement cafés and restaurants that make the Zona Velha the bustling heart of Funchal's nightlife. Many restaurants specialize in fresh fish, and it is to here that Portuguese holiday-makers come for *bacalhau* (salt cod) or *arroz de mariscos* (seafood risotto). Several restaurants also offer *fado* music, that strangely plaintive and addictive import from the back streets of Lisbon in which the singer bemoans their star-crossed fate.

✚ 142 F3 ✉ Located in the eastern part of the city ¶ Some of the city's best restaurants are here (€–€€)

Exploring

Madeira has never quite lost its image of being an island retreat for those in delicate health, a place where the bankrupt old nobility of Europe could flee to escape their debts, or a retirement home for impoverished former colonial servants. Young travellers turn up their noses at the thought of a destination with no beaches, and no nightlife.

It is, however, one of Europe's most intriguing destinations. The island's mountainous volcanic landscape is carved into scores of deep valleys and ravines, clothed in the luxuriant vegetation that thrives in the frost-free climate. Hundreds of miles of footpaths run alongside the network of irrigation canals *(levadas)*, bringing water from the wet side of the island to the drier south. Easy to follow, these paths lead you deep into the rural heart of the island, where the way of life has hardly caught up with the industrial era.

Funchal

**Funchal means 'fennel' and the
city's name is said to derive from
the abundance of fennel plants
that Zarco, the island's discoverer,
found growing here when he arrived in 1420.**

High above the harbour, on the clifftops west of the city, is the
Hotel Zone, where most visitors to Madeira stay. The area is
almost a self-contained town, with its tourist shops and
supermarkets, its lido complex and restaurants. Downtown
Funchal is split into three sectors by its rivers, now enclosed
between high embankments to prevent the flash floods that
previously claimed several lives.

In the eastern sector of the city is the Zona Velha, or Old Town
(➤ 40–41), with its many restaurants. The central sector contains a
jumble of embroidery
factories, crumbling
town houses and
shops selling pungent
salt cod and dried
herbs. Most of
Funchal's cultural sights
are packed into the
maze of streets in the
westernmost third of
the city, focused
around two of
Madeira's oldest
buildings, the Sé
(➤ 38–39) and the
Alfândega Velha (Old
Customs House),
now the Madeiran
parliament building.

ADEGAS DE SÃO FRANCISCO

See pages 22–23.

CONVENTO DE SANTA CLARA

High walls surround the Convent of the Poor Clares, shutting off from the world Madeira's oldest religious foundation. Santa Clara was founded in 1496 by João Gonçalves de Câmara, one of the grandsons of Zarco, the discoverer of Madeira. Zarco's granddaughter, Dona Isabella, was installed as the first abbess, establishing a tradition of aristocratic patronage that ensured that the convent was richly endowed. Many a daughter of wealthy parents was forced to take the veil on reaching her eighteenth birthday, a practice that was supposed to confer spiritual benefits on both parents and child. The convent became a popular tourist attraction in the 19th century, when visitors would come ostensibly to buy flowers made of feathers and sample sweetmeats made by the nuns, but in reality hoping to catch sight of some legendary beauty, tragically cut off from the delights of the world.

Today the nuns run a well-regarded kindergarten. Ring the bell on the gate and you will be given a guided tour of the chapels that lie off the peaceful 15th-century cloisters. The chapels shelter an astonishing wealth of paintings, sculpture and *azulejos* tiles, and in due course these will be housed in a new museum. The church alongside is on the site of a 15th-century chapel where the island's first three governors, including Zarco, were buried. Glazed *azulejos* decorate the domed church tower, and there are more ancient tiles, faded but still impressive, covering the walls. Above is a typical Madeiran church ceiling of timber, painted with floral patterns and a galleon in full sail.

✚ 142 A1 ✉ Calçada de Santa Clara ☎ 742 602 🕐 Mon–Sat 10–12, 3–5; Sun 10–12; ring for entry if door is closed, but not over the lunch period
✋ Moderate ⬌ Museu Freitas (➤ 58–59), Museu Municipal (➤ 59)

FORTALEZA DE SÃO TIAGO

Attracted by stories of Madeira's massive sugar-derived wealth, French, English, Algerian and Turkish pirates regularly attacked Funchal from the 16th century, looting churches and wine cellars and killing anyone who stood in their way. In response, Madeira's governor ordered the construction of massive walls and fortifications, which were extended and reinforced over a 100-year period. Built in 1614, the Fortress of St James was one of the last fortifications to be completed. It is also the only fort fully open to the public, since the others are still used by the Portuguese military. Newly restored, the building now houses a museum of contemporary art, but the rather unexciting works on display are a distraction from the real interest of the fortress – the maze of passages, staircases and towers, which make a perfect playground for children, and the views over the rooftops of Funchal to be had from the ramparts.

✚ 142 F3 ✉ Rua do Portão de São Tiago ☎ 213 340 ◉ Mon–Sat 10–12.30, 2–5.30. Closed Sun, public hols ✋ Moderate 🍴 Restaurant (€€); eat lunch here and admission to the fortress is free ↔ Zona Velha (➤ 40–41)

IBTAM HANDICRAFTS INSTITUTE

IBTAM is the body that oversees standards in Madeira's economically important embroidery industry, and the small museum on the first floor of its headquarters building is a showcase for Madeiran handicrafts. The rather drab and old-fashioned displays are brought to life by the vibrant colours of traditional island costume, including scarlet and yellow skirts, waistcoats and scarves. Also on display are intricately embroidered tablecloths and bedspreads, and diaphanous nightgowns. On the staircase leading up to the museum is an impressive tapestry depicting a flower-filled Madeiran landscape, made in 1958–61 and comprising some 7 million stitches.

✚ 142 E1 ✉ Rua do Visconde de Anadia 44 ☎ 223 141 ⏰ Mon–Fri 10–12.30, 2.30–5.30. Closed Sat, Sun, public hols ✋ Moderate ↔ Museu Franco (➤ 56–57)

JARDIM BOTÂNICO

Nineteenth-century writers bestowed many fanciful names on Madeira to describe the island's botanical wealth – 'a floating greenhouse' and 'God's botanical garden' being among them. The first plant seeds were probably carried by oceanic currents from West Africa, or reached Madeira in bird droppings. Thriving in the island's fertile volcanic soil, species evolved that are unique to the island. Early settlers may have destroyed many more plants as they slashed and burned the island's dense vegetation. Zarco ordered the island's woods to be set alight, and such was the ferocity of the resulting blaze that the explorers were driven back to their ships, eventually being forced to put out to sea to escape the heat.

Even so, it is unlikely that the whole island was burned, for several large areas of wilderness remain on Madeira, and the Botanical Garden displays examples of the kind of trees and shrubs that make up Madeira's virgin forest. Among them is the dragon tree, with its smooth bark and claw-like leaf clusters, valued since ancient times for its red sap used for cloth dyeing.

Competing with the dragon tree are the many strange and colourful

plants introduced to Madeira from far-distant lands, all displayed here in a series of terraced beds. Stars of the show include the tropical orchids (in flower from November to March), while other beds are devoted to the plants that underpin Madeira's cut-flower trade – such as bird of paradise plants and arum lilies – and a fine collection of cacti and sculptural agaves.

➕ 138 E1 ✉ Quinta do Bom Sucesso, Caminho do Meio ☎ 211 200 🕐 Daily 9–5.30. Closed public hols
🖐 Moderate (includes entrance to nearby Jardim dos Loiros ➤ below) 🍴 Café (€) in grounds 🚌 Town bus 31 or cable car from Monte

JARDIM DOS LOIROS

Exotic screeches, whoops and squawks advertise the presence of this tropical bird garden, where even the brightest flowers are put in the shade by the plumage of cockatoos, parrots and macaws. Children will enjoy the antics of the birds, which are displayed in aviaries dotted around the gardens.

➕ 138 E1 ✉ Caminho do Meio ☎ 211 200 🕐 Daily 9–5.30. Closed public hols
🖐 Moderate (includes entrance to nearby Jardim Botânico; ➤ above)
🚌 Town bus 31 or cable car from Monte

JARDIM DE SANTA CATARINA

This public park is named after the Chapel of St Catherine, founded in 1425 by Constança Rodriguez, wife of Zarco. The little chapel, with its attractive porch and holy water stoup, stands on a terrace from which there are good views of the harbour.

Elsewhere the park is dotted with sculptures, ranging from a modernist fountain featuring a female torso to the vigorous bronze figure of the Semeador, the Sower (1919), by Francisco Franco. The Sower metaphorically broadcasts his seed across immaculate flower beds, and the upper part of the garden, with its aviaries and children's playground, has many fine tropical flowering trees. From the park, you can walk uphill into the well-tended and shady grounds of the Quinta Vigia, the pink-painted mansion that forms the official residence of Madeira's president. On the opposite side of the road is the Hospicio da Princesa, built as a tuberculosis sanatorium in 1859, with another fine garden featuring several ancient dragon trees.

🔢 142 A4 ✉ Avenida do Infante 🕐 24 hours ♿ Free 🍴 Café (€) in grounds ↔ Adegas de São Francisco (➤ 22–23)

MADEIRA STORY CENTRE

The Madeira Story Centre, in the Old Town (Zona Velha), is a great place to go early in your visit to Madeira for an overview of the island's history. The exhibits appeal to children as well as adults, with touch-screen interactive quizzes, ferocious French pirates and even a few smells. Crammed into the main exhibition area are maps, astrolabes and models of the ships that carried early settlers from Portugal to Madeira, a working model of a sugar mill and screens showing Pathé News film footage from the 1950s

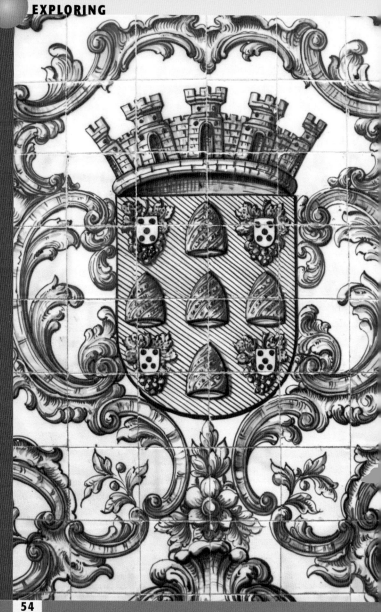

and 1960s. A mock-up of an Aquila Airways airline cabin hints at the luxury enjoyed by passengers on seaplane flights between Southampton and Funchal from 1949 to 1958, with Winston Churchill, and Gregory Peck (star of *Moby Dick*, filmed in Madeira in 1956) among the passengers.

➕ 142 E3 ✉ Rua Dom Carlos I 27–29 🕐 Daily 9–7. Closed 25 Dec ✋ Expensive

MERCADO DOS LAVRADORES
See pages 28–29.

MUSEU 'A CIDADE DO AÇÚCAR'
This history museum has been erected around the excavated remains of a house built in 1495 for Jeanin Esmerandt, a Flemish merchant working for the Bruges-based Company Despars. The significance of the house is that Christopher Columbus twice stayed here as a guest of Esmerandt: once in 1480, and again in 1498 (after his pioneering voyage across the Atlantic to the Americas) when he stayed for six days. The original house was demolished in 1876 and excavated in 1989. Finds from the excavation exhibited here include pottery, food remains (nuts, seashells and animal bones), jewellery, coins and bone buttons. Also on display here are ceramic sugar cones, similar to those which feature on Funchal's coat of arms, and 16th-century engravings of the sugar-making process. The enormous wealth that sugar brought to Funchal is represented here by religious paintings and statues acquired by the city's merchants.

➕ 142 C2 ✉ Praça do Colombo ☎ 236 910 🕐 Mon–Fri 10–12.30, 2–6. Closed Sat, Sun, public hols ✋ Moderate 🍴 Cafés (€) in nearby Largo da Sé (cathedral square) ↔ Museu de Arte Sacra (➤ 32–33)

MUSEU DE ARTE SACRA
See pages 32–33.

MUSEU FRANCO

This quiet and little-visited museum celebrates the artistic achievements of two brothers born on Madeira but who achieved fame on the wider European stage. Henrique Franco (1883–1961) was a painter and his older brother Francisco (1855–1955) was a sculptor. Both studied in Paris, where they were friendly with Picasso, Degas and Modigliani, but their careers were largely centred on the Portuguese capital, Lisbon.

The first part of the museum is devoted to a series of Gauginesque portraits, painted by Henrique. He often painted his subjects – from weather-beaten peasants to industrialists and aristocrats – against a colourful background of flowers and foliage reminiscent of the Madeiran landscape.

Francisco's vigorous but monochrome sculptures in the second part of the museum are evidence of a busy life devoted to designing public memorials, coins, medals and postage stamps, including such sculptures as the Zarco monument in central Funchal and the *Semeador* in the Jardim de Santa Catarina (➤ 52).

➕ 142 E1 ✉ Rua João de Deus 13
☎ 230 633 🕐 Mon–Fri 10–12.30, 2–6. Closed Sat, Sun, public hols ✋ Moderate 🍴 Pavement cafés and coffee bars abound in Praça do Carmo, off Rua das Hortas (two blocks south of the museum) ↔ IBTAM Handicrafts Institute (➤ 49)

MUSEU FREITAS

Halfway up the steep and cobbled Calçada de Santa Clara is this balconied town house, whose stately rooms provide a glimpse of life on Madeira at any time over the last 150 years.

The first part of the museum consists of a gallery covering the history of *azulejos* tiles, those brightly coloured ceramics that decorate church walls all over Madeira, as well as domestic homes. Originating in the Islamic east, the practice of using tiles spread from Persia to Portugal via Moorish North Africa and Spain. Madeira lacked suitable clays to produce its own tiles so imported them from Seville in the 16th century, then from the Netherlands. Examples of tiles from Santa Clara convent are among the earliest exhibits, while the last flowering of tile manufacture includes some lovely art nouveau ones.

The second part of the museum consists of the house bequeathed to Funchal by Dr Frederico de Freitas, in 1978. It dates back to the late 17th century. A conservatory in the garden, a glass-roofed winter garden and art nouveau furnishing all lend charm to a house crammed with fascinating objects collected by Dr Freitas during his world travels. The collections include oriental carpets, religious paintings, *azulejos* and fine antique furnishings, as well as

17th- and 18th-century hand-carved crib figures originating from mainland Portugal and the Portuguese colonies of Goa and Macau.
✚ 142 A2 ✉ Calçada de Santa Clara 7 ☎ 220 578 🕒 Tue–Sat 10–12.30, 2–5.30, Sun 10–12.30. Closed Mon, public hols ✋ Moderate ↔ Convento de Santa Clara (➤ 46), Museu Municipal (➤ below)

MUSEU MUNICIPAL

The Municipal Museum has a tiny aquarium on the ground floor stocked with the fish that are typically caught off Madeiran shores, including grouper fish, moray eels and bottom-dwelling flounders. Upstairs is a collection of stuffed birds and animals, including sharks with gaping jaws and giant crabs with metre-long claws. Displays of Madeiran birds are as close as you are likely to get to the more elusive species that nest on inaccessible cliffs.
✚ 142 A2 ✉ Rua da Mouraria 31 ☎ 229 761 🕒 Tue–Fri 10–6, Sat, Sun, public hols 12–6. Closed Mon, 25 Dec, 1 Jan ✋ Moderate ↔ Convento de Santa Clara (➤ 46), Museu Freitas (➤ above)

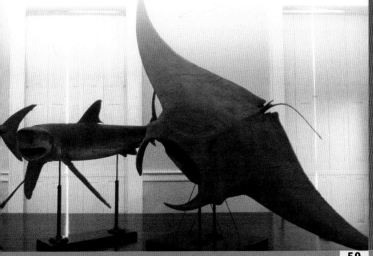

a walk

exploring Funchal's architecture

Discover Funchal's rich architectural heritage on a stroll through the city centre.

Start at the Câmara Municipal (Town Hall).

The elegant 18th-century mansion was built for the Count of Carvalhal but sold by his profligate heirs. The delightful palm-filled courtyard features a graceful sculpture of *Leda and the Swan* (1880). Turn your back on the entrance to view Praça do Município (Town Square), paved with grey basalt and white marble in a fish-scale pattern. To the right, gesticulating saints decorate the façade of the Igreja di Colégio, the Jesuit church, founded in 1574. To the left is the Bishop's Palace of 1600, now housing the Museu de Arte Sacra (Sacred Art Museum ➤ 32–33).

Cross the square, heading for the far right-hand corner. Walk up shop-lined Rua C Pestana and carry straight on at the next junction, along traffic-free Rua da Carreira.

Three doors up on the left, in Rua da Carreira, is the entrance to the Pátio complex, with its courtyard café and Vicentes photographic museum (➤ 62–63). Try coffee here, or buy typical Madeiran *bolo de mel* (literally 'honey cake' but actually made with molasses) at the baker's further up on the left.

Walk up Rua da Carreira.

As you dip in and out of the street's characterful shops, look up to see the pretty wrought-iron balconies that decorate many of the upper storeys. Among the best houses is No 155.

The third turn right (Rua do Quebra Costas) leads to the English Church (completed 1822), set in a pretty garden.

At the end of Rua da Carreira is the British Cemetery (Cimitero Inglesa), the burial ground of Madeira's Protestants of all nationalities, worth visiting for its many poignant 19th-century memorials and epitaphs.

Distance 1km (half mile)
Time 30 minutes
Start point Câmara Municipal (Town Hall), Praça do Município
➕ 142 C2
End point British Cemetery, Rua da Carreira. To enter the cemetery, ring the bell at No 235
Lunch O Pátio Café (€) ✉ Rua da Carreira 43 ☎ 227 376

O PÁTIO

O Pátio (The Patio) is a charming building dating from the 1860s, consisting of a courtyard and café, open to the sky, shaded by palms and surrounded by an arcade of small shops. Rising from the cobbled court-yard is an ornate double staircase with wrought-iron balustrades, leading up to a fanciful balcony of similar design, looking like a saloon bar in some Wild West movie.

The upper floor houses the photo-graphic studio of Vicente Gomes da Silva, founded in 1865, when the art of photography was still relatively new. In fact, this was the first commercial photographic studio to be established in Portugal; such was the demand for holiday souvenirs from wealthy visitors to Madeira that Gomes da Silva felt confident in pouring a small fortune into the purchase of mahogany and brass-bound plate cameras, together with all the paraphernalia of the darkroom. Visitors to the studio can browse through a selection of the 380,000 or so photographs that have survived in the Vicentes collection, a rich resource covering nearly 140 years of island history, and look at a collection of antique cameras, costumes and studio props.

➕ 142 B2 ✉ Rua da Carreira 43 ☎ 225 050 (museum); 227 376 (café)
🕐 Patio: daily 9–6. Museum: Tue–Sat 10–12.30, 2–5. Closed Sun, Mon and public hols ↔ Museu Municipal (➤ 59)

PICO (CASTELO DO PICO)

It is a sweaty, heart-pounding climb up to the Pico, or Radio Peak as it is known locally because of the naval communications masts bristling from its heights. It is worth the effort for the *castelo*, built in 1632–40 to warn of sea attack. A walk around the walls is rewarding for the views down across Funchal's rooftops and up to the wooded heights above the city. A small exhibition room in the castle traces its history through old engravings.

➕ 138 E1 ✉ Rua do Castelo 🕐 Daily 9–6 ✋ Free ↔ Quinta das Cruzes (➤ 64)

QUINTA DAS CRUZES

Of the many fine mansions built by wealthy merchants around Funchal, the Quinta das Cruzes (the Mansion of the Crosses) is the only one open to the public. Zarco, the discoverer of Madeira and the island's first governor, built his house on this site in the 1450s, but little remains from this era except for some architectural fragments displayed in the gardens. These include gravestones, crosses and broken pieces of church fonts, as well as all that remains of Funchal's pillory, where miscreants were once publicly flogged. Most striking of all are two stone window frames, carved with dancing figures and man-eating lions in the style known as Manueline, after the reigning monarch.

The present house dates from the 17th century, when it was built for the Lomelino family, wealthy wine merchants from Genova. Furnished in the Empire style, which was popular at the time, the rooms are arranged thematically, with sections devoted to oriental art, French porcelain, topographical views and portraits, costume and crib figures.

The basement contains an unusual collection of furniture made from recycled packing cases. Sugar was once so precious that it was shipped in chests made from best Brazilian satinwood. Once competition from the New World destroyed Madeira's sugar trade, enterprising cabinetmakers reused the wood to make the fine cupboards displayed here.

✚ 142 A1 ✉ Calçada do Pico 1 ☎ 740 670 🕓 Tue–Sat 10–12.30, 2–5.30, Sun 10–1. Closed Mon, public hols 🖐 Moderate ↔ Convento de Santa Clara (► 46)

SÉ (CATHEDRAL)
See pages 38–39.

ZONA VELHA (OLD TOWN)
See pages 40–41.

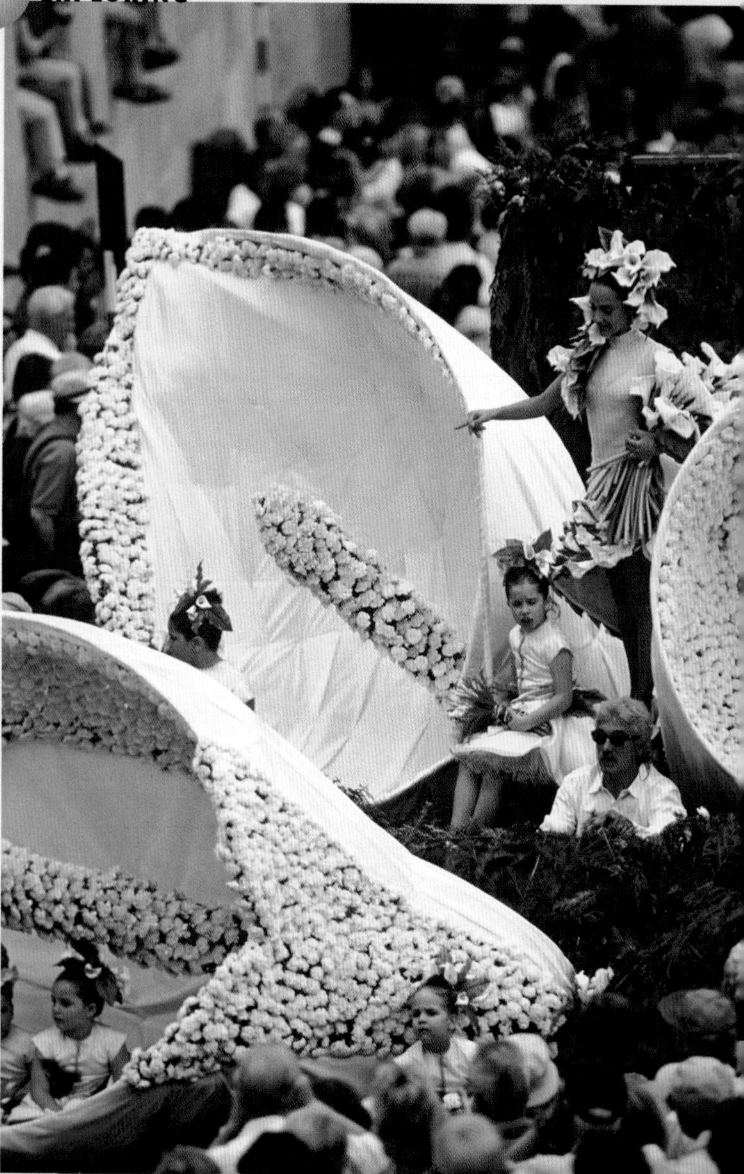

Western Madeira

The western third of Madeira used to be the least accessible: just getting to Ribeira Brava, the starting point for exploring the west, took more than an hour from Funchal. However, in 1997 transport on the island was revolutionized with the opening of the Via Rápida expressway, so that Ribeira Brava is now only 15 minutes' drive away. From here you can explore picturesque fishing villages, bleak moorland and mountains cloaked in dense forest.

The south coast is one long ribbon of vineyards and banana plantations, with steep lanes linking one hamlet to the next. By contrast, the north coast road offers some of the most dramatic scenery on the island, with the boiling ocean dashing against huge black rocks and waterfalls cascading from clifftop to sea.

BOCA DA ENCUMEADA

The Boca da Encumeada (Encumeada Pass), midway between Ribeira Brava and São Vicente, is a popular stopping-off point for round-the-island tours because of the extensive views from the lookout point at the top. Weather permitting, you can see across to São Vicente on the north coast and down the Serra de Água Valley to the south coast, though more often than not you will stand in brilliant sunshine looking down over rain clouds.

If the weather is fine and clear, follow the Levada do Norte (Levada of the North) westwards: look for the sign to Folhadal opposite the café and climb up to the *levada* past the keeper's house. It is worth exploring this path for 2km (1.2 miles) or so; you will find an abundance of wild flowers and excellent views south.

✚ 137 B6 ✉ On EN 104 road, 43km (27 miles) northwest of Funchal
🍴 Snack bar (€) alongside the viewpoint car park; for more substantial meals

try the restaurant in the Residencial (€€, ☎ 951 282), 2km (1.2 miles) south on the road to Serra de Água 🚌 139

CALHETA

Calheta is the main town for the southwestern coast of Madeira. Every front garden hosts a colourful display of scarlet and pink geraniums, mauve bougainvillaea and purple passion flowers. If you come here on 7th or 8th September even the streets are covered in flowers as carpets of blooms are laid out to celebrate the Feast of Our Lady of Loreto.

Like most of the island's churches, Calheta's has been rebuilt many times and looks disappointingly modern at first, but inside is a large tabernacle of ebony and silver, donated by Portugal's King Manuel I (1469–1521). The sanctuary has a fine wooden ceiling in the Moorish-influenced *mudejar* style. The sweet smell of cane syrup from the factory next door may tempt you to take a tour to watch rum and molasses being produced.

It is worth seeking out two more churches. At Loreto (east of Calheta), the church has a south portal carved in the lively Manueline style typical of the early 16th century, and a *mudejar*-style wooden ceiling.

The best church in the area is the Capela dos Reis Magos (Chapel of the Three Kings) at Lombo dos Reis (between Estreito da Calheta and Jardim do Mar, west of Calheta). Here the chapel houses a rare wooden reredos, carved in Antwerp in the 16th century with a lively scene depicting the Adoration of the Magi.

✚ 132 F3 ✉ On south coast, 61km (38 miles) west of Funchal 🍴 Marisqueria Rocha Mar (€€), east of town, on coast road to Madalena do Mar; renowned for seafood 🚌 80, 107 ❓ Sugar mill (☎ 822 264) open daily during working hours, except public hols

PAÚL DA SERRA

Flat, bleak and grazed by hardy free-range cows, sheep and goats, the Paúl da Serra comes as a surprise to travellers grown used to views of jagged mountain peaks. This windswept plateau offers expansive views of moorland, its wild open landscape somewhat compromised by a forest of wind turbines, built to supply electricity to the communities of the island's northern coast. Even so, it is worth coming here to look for wild bilberries in autumn and to savour the eerie atmosphere, or to enjoy the panoramic views to be had when the plateau is not enshrouded in cloud.

➕ 133 E6 ✉ 61km (38 miles) northwest of Funchal, either side of the EN 124

PONTA DO PARGO

Visitors are drawn to the westernmost tip of Madeira by the thought that nothing now stands between them and the east coast of America except for hundreds of miles of ocean. Standing alongside the clifftop lighthouse at Ponta do Pargo, 300m (985ft) above the sea, you can try spotting fishermen who come here to catch the *pargos* (dolphin fish, no relation to the dolphin) after which Ponta do Pargo (Dolphin Point) is named. You can also pick up the Levada Calheta–Ponta do Pargo, the water channel that runs parallel to the south coast, weaving in and out of the hills as it follows the 650m (2,130ft) contour with views south to the sea and north to the Paúl da Serra plateau. Frequent bus services pass along the nearby EN 101 road, so you can park in Ponta do Pargo, walk as far as you choose and then catch a bus back to your car.

➕ 132 C1 ✉ 77km (48 miles) west of Funchal 🍽 Casa de Chá O Fío (€) on the headland above the lighthouse 🚌 80, 107, 142

PONTA DO SOL

Sunset is a good time
to visit Ponta do Sol for
uninterrupted views of
the western sky while
strolling along the
harbour promenade.
Steep cobbled streets
lead upwards to the
church, with its unusual
green ceramic font,
donated by King
Manuel I (1469–1521),
and its ancient wooden
ceilings, painted with
scenes from the Life of
the Virgin. Behind the
church, a plaque on the
wall of the John dos Passos Cultural Centre, at Rua Príncipe
D Luís I, records a visit made by John dos Passos (1896–1970), the
American novelist whose grandparents emigrated from this village
in the mid-19th century. The Centre has changing exhibitions and
occasional dance and theatre performances.

The church at nearby Madalena do Mar (sadly always locked) is
the burial place of an intriguing figure known as Henrique Alemão
(Henry the German) – in reality King Wladyslaw III of Poland, who
chose self-imposed exile on Madeira after losing the Battle of
Varna in 1414. Here he became a prosperous farmer and built
a chapel on the site of today's church. Tragically, Wladyslaw
drowned near Cabo Girão (➤ 24–25) as his ship hit rocks on
the way to Lisbon to see King Manuel I.

➕ 136 D3 ✉ 42km (26 miles) west of Funchal 🍴 A Poente (€) on the cliff at
the eastern end of the seafront is well positioned for sunset views (☎ 973
579) 🚌 4, 80, 107, 115, 142, 146

PORTO DO MONIZ

Porto do Moniz is a surprisingly cosmopolitan place for a village located at the northernmost extremity of Madeira, thanks to the waterfront hotels and restaurants catering for travellers on round-the-island tours. Bones weary from walking or jolting up and down the island's roads can be revived by a good soaking in the natural rock pools of the town's new bathing complex. These pools have been enlarged to create a warm sea-water bathing area, just a few feet away from the Atlantic waves that crash against Madeira's northern shore. The waves carry salt-laden spray far up into the surrounding hills, hence the ingenious use of grass and bracken fences to protect the crops growing in the fields surrounding the village. Viewed from the steep roads descending into the village,

this patchwork of tiny fields and fences creates an attractive pattern.

Other attractions in Porto do Moniz include a small aquarium on the seafront and the Living Science Centre nearby, which hosts changing exhibitions.

✚ 132 A4 ✉ 75km (47 miles) northwest of Funchal 🍴 Good choice of restaurants (€€), including the Cachalote (€€, ☎ 853 180), specializing in seafood 🚌 80, 139

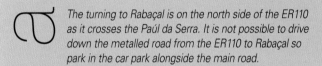

a walk along the Levada do Risco

If you are driving across the Paúl da Serra, it is well worth breaking your journey to explore this secret valley of ancient trees and mossy waterfalls.

The turning to Rabaçal is on the north side of the ER110 as it crosses the Paúl da Serra. It is not possible to drive down the metalled road from the ER110 to Rabaçal so park in the car park alongside the main road.

Follow the winding track downhill for 2km (1.2 miles) until you come to the government rest house (with public facilities such as barbecue pits, picnic tables and toilets).

Follow the sign to the right of the rest house down the track to the Levada do Risco.

The Levada do Risco watercourse is cut into a hillside cloaked in huge gnarled tree heathers. The humid air has encouraged the growth of magnificent lichens, some resembling apple-coloured seaweed.

After five minutes' walking, a path leads left, signposted Levada das 25 Fontes (the Levada of the 25 Springs). Ignore this for now and carry straight on.

After another ten minutes' easy walking you will come to the Risco waterfall, pouring down from the rocky heights into a magical fern-hung bowl. To your left there are sweeping views down into the green valley of the River Janela, which this waterfall feeds.

Return the way you came. You can extend your walk by taking the slightly more difficult Levada das 25 Fontes, following the signposted path downhill and then turning right once you reach the levada. This will take you, after a 20-minute walk, to another fine waterfall with one main cascade and many smaller ones.

Distance 7km (4 miles)
Time 2–3 hours
Start/end point Rabaçal turning, on the ER110 ✠ 133 D5
Lunch No cafés in the area; take a picnic

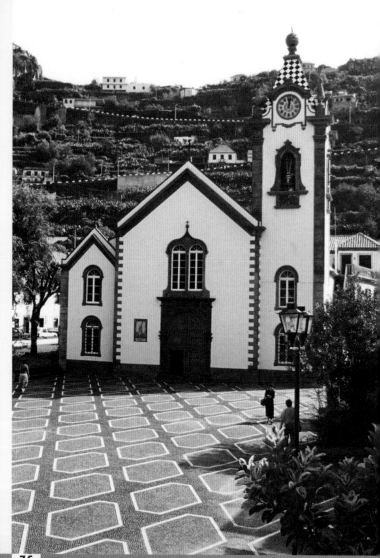

RIBEIRA BRAVA

To understand why Ribeira Brava (Wild River) is so named, you have to visit in late autumn or winter, when the river that runs through the town centre is in full spate. For the rest of the year its harmless appearance belies its true nature. Over several thousand millennia this river has carved out a deep cleft that seems almost to divide Madeira in two, running due north from Ribeira Brava up to the Encumeada Pass and on to São Vicente, on the north coast of Madeira. The road that runs up this valley has long been an important transport route, which is why Ribeira Brava has grown into a sizeable town, with a market and a number of seafront cafés where farmers, taking their produce to Funchal, stop to break their journey.

Just back from the seafront is the splendid Church of São Bento (St Benedict). Like most churches on Madeira it has been rebuilt many times, but there are several features remaining from the original 15th-century church, including the painted font, decorated with grapes, pomegranates and wild beasts, and the carved stone pulpit. The right-hand chapel contains a fine Flemish painting of the Nativity, surrounded by gilded woodwork. At the north end of town, the Museu Etnográfico da Madeira (Madeira Ethnographic Museum) offers displays on fishing, agriculture, weaving and winemaking.

✠ 136 D4 ✉ 32km (20 miles) west of Funchal ⑪ Good choice of cafés and restaurants (€–€€) along the seafront road, and along the cobbled main street, Rua do Visconde 🚌 7

ℹ Tourist office (☎ 951 675), in the Forte de São Bento, along the seafront road

Museu Etnográfico da Madeira

✉ Rua de São Francisco 24 ☎ 952 598 ⏰ Tue–Sun 10–12.30, 2–6

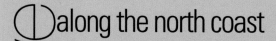

along the north coast

Much of the excitement of driving along the corniche that links Porto do Moniz (▶ 73) and São Vicente has been dimished now that a new road has been built, enclosed within tunnels for much of its length.

However, you can still drive parts of the old road, provided you travel in a westerly direction (it is now strictly a one-way road). Badly maintained as it is, you can still enjoy one of Europe's most spectacular roads, built on a narrow shelf cut into the cliff face high above the raging sea (drive slowly and with great care).

You will want to slow down, in any event, in order to take in the spectacular coastal views. At several points, waterfalls will come cascading down on top of your car – frightening as the noise can be, Madeirans look on the positive side: 'It's a free car wash', they say.

Halfway along the route you will find the village of Seixal (▶ 82), worth a stop to stretch your legs and enjoy the views of vineyards clinging to the slopes behind the village. The grapes grown here go to produce the rich dry Seixal variety of Madeira wine. West of the village, a side road leads down to rock pools and concrete terraces designed for swimming.

Distance 18km (11 miles)
Time 45 minutes
Start point São Vicente ✚ 133 C7
End point Porto do Moniz ✚ 132 A4
Lunch O Virgilio (€€) ✉ On the seafront at São Vicente ☎ 842 467

SÃO VICENTE

São Vicente, a prosperous agricultural town, caters to travellers exploring Madeira's northern coast. The historic core has traffic-free streets lined with shops, tubs brimming with flowers and houses painted a dazzling white. In the 17th-century church, the painted ceiling and carved altar show St Vincent blessing the town.

About 1.25km (0.75 mile) south of São Vicente, on the road to Lameiros, you will find the **Grutas de São Vicente**. The 30-minute guided tour of the lava-tube caves is extremely popular, particulary with children. At the adjacent Centro do Volcanismo visitor centre audiovisual displays explain the island's volcanic history, giving an insight into how the caves were formed.

A short, worthwhile walk along the Levada da Fajã do Rodrigues can be found about 3.5km (2 miles) south along the road to Serra

de Água. Take the second of two right turns signposted to Ginjas, and take the next left (signposted Parque Empresarial de São Vicente). After 2km (1.2 miles), take a left (signposted Miradouro) and continue until you come to the Parque. Take the uppermost of the park roads and look for the concreted path that leads up to a forest post and picnic area. The walk starts 100m (330ft) above the picnic area, reached by a rough track that runs up to a large reservoir on the right. Turn right to follow the *levada* for 1km (half mile) to reach a spectacular *caldeirão*.

✚ 133 C7 ✉ 55km (34 miles) north of Funchal 🍴 Good choice of cafés and restaurants (€–€€) ☎ 842 467) 🚍 6, 132, 139

Grutas e Centro do Volcanismo de São Vicente

✉ Sítio do Pé do Passo, São Vicente ☎ 842 404 ⏰ Apr–Sep daily 9–9; Oct–Mar daily 9–7 💷 Expensive

SEIXAL

Seixal, midway between Porto do Moniz and São Vicente, is a good spot at which to break your journey along the north coast road (► 78). Here you can explore the rocky foreshore (follow the signs to Piscina for a group of big, sheltered rock pools) and walk out along the jetty for views of the coastal cliffs and waterfalls which rise up on either side of the tiny village, really little more than a hamlet. Excellent wine is produced locally from grapes grown in tiny vineyards clinging to the cliffs and protected from the wind and salt spray by fences constructed from dried bracken and tree heather. Grapes grown here are used in the driest of the four main types of Madeira wine.

🚹 133 B5 ⊠ 61km (38 miles) northwest of Funchal 🍴 Local wine and snacks at bar of Estalagem Brisamar guest house (€€, ☎ 854 476) 🚌 139

Central Madeira

Central Madeira combines both the suburban sprawl of Funchal and the cinder-strewn volcanic landscape of the island's central mountain range. Though they are only 30 minutes' drive apart, one is rarely visible from the other since more often than not cloud obscures the mountain peaks.

The mountains are easy enough to reach, thanks to the road that goes to the top of Pico do Arieiro, Madeira's third highest peak. Once there, paths invite exploration of the endless series of knife-edge ridges that extend to the horizon in every direction. Beyond the central mountain range, the north side of the island is dotted with tiny hamlets surrounded by a patchwork of terraced fields and orchards, plantations producing willow for basket-making, and thatched cow byres.

CABO GIRÃO
See pages 24–25.

CÂMARA DE LOBOS
The much-photographed fishing village of Câmara de Lobos owes its appeal to the small fleet of fishing boats based here, brightly painted in primary colours and drawn up on the town's small pebble beach for much of the day. On the eastern side of the harbour there is a small boatyard where you can watch boats being made and repaired. Local fishermen go out at night to catch *espada* (scabbard fish), which live at depths of 800m (2,625ft) or more (hence their big eyes, needed to see in the gloom). At night they come up to feed, and that is when they are most easily caught, using long lines, each with 150 or so hooks, baited with squid.

To see the catch being brought in you need to be up early: by 7am most of the fish will have been cleaned and despatched to Funchal market. The fishermen, meanwhile, celebrate the night's catch by filling the local bars. You are likely to encounter some poverty in the village, especially in the alleys leading west from the harbour, where large families live in tiny single-roomed houses, crammed up against the cliff face. Here you will also find the simple fishermen's chapel, its walls painted with naïve

scenes showing the Life of St Anthony, including a storm-tossed ship in which he sailed from Italy to Portugal, and a sermon he preached that was so eloquent even the fish gathered to listen – both appropriate subjects for a fishing village.

✚ 137 E7 ✉ 14km (8.5 miles) west of Funchal 🍴 Good choice of cafés and restaurants (€–€€), including Churchill's (€€, ☎ 941 541), on the east side of the harbour 🚌 Most westbound buses go to Câmara de Lobos, including 4, 6, 107, 154

CURRAL DAS FREIRAS

See pages 26–27.

FAIAL

Faial is worth a brief stop for the views to be had from the *miradouro* (viewpoint) overlooking the Ametade Valley, west of the village. In the centre of the village is the new bridge that replaced one swept away in flash floods in 1980, spanning the Ribeira Séca (Dry River), which lives up to its name most of the time but can rise to a raging torrent with the autumn rains. The *miradouro* west of the village is the best spot to take in the gaunt heights of Penha de Águia (Eagle Rock), the peak that overshadows Faial, rising sheer from the sea to a height of 590m (1,935ft).

✚ 135 D5 ✉ 30km (18.5 miles) north of Funchal 🍴 Casa de Chá do Faial at Lombo do Baixo, on the EN 103 south of Faial; good views 🚌 53, 78

a walk up Pico Ruivo

Getting to the top of Madeira's highest peak does not require exceptional skills in mountaineering since there is a good paved path all the way to the summit, but you do need to carry a light jacket as it can be cold on the mountain top, and you should take adequate precautions against sunburn.

Start early for the best panoramas: by the middle of the morning warm air rising from the coastal regions will have condensed on meeting the colder air of the mountains, forming clouds that, although lending their own charm to the scene, limit the views.

To reach the path, drive from Santana (▶ 94–97) along the EN 101-5 to the car park and rest house where the road runs out at Achada do Teixeira (1,592m/5,223ft).

Just behind the rest house is the curious rock formation known as Homem em Pé (Man on Foot), a group of eroded basalt dykes.

The well-trodden path to Pico Ruivo (Red Peak) leads west from here. After some 45 minutes, the path divides; take the path to the right up through a gate and on to the government rest house, a prominent white building. Two minutes on, the path divides and you take the left fork.

From here it is a scramble over rough boulder steps to the Pico Ruivo summit (1,861m/6,454ft), but the effort is well worth while for the breathtaking views of the central mountain range, and of the island of Porto Santo (▶ 117–127), floating in the sea away to the northeast.

Distance 3.5km (2 miles)

Time 2 hours

Start/end point Achada do Teixeira rest house ✚ 134 D3 🚌 Taxi required

Lunch Nearest café is in Santana; drinks (coffee, beer, cola etc) can be bought at the rest house just below the summit (open only in high season)

MONTE

High above Funchal, the hill town of Monte is easily reached thanks to the cable car that now runs from the Zona Velha (► 40–41). A second cable car also links Monte with the Jardim Botânico (► 50–51).

Apart from the famous Monte toboggan ride (► 30–31), there are several reasons to come to Monte. One is to visit the Church of Nossa Senhora (Our Lady), whose spotlit façade is a prominent landmark at night, visible on the hillside high above Funchal. Fronting the church is a flight of 74 steps. Penitents scramble up these on their knees during the festivities for the Feast of the Assumption (15 August). Inside the church is a statue of the Virgin housed in a silver tabernacle. It is said that the 15th-century statue was given to a Madeiran shepherd girl by the Virgin herself, and it is credited with many miracles. The north chapel contains the imposing black coffin of the Emperor Charles I, who died of pneumonia on Madeira in 1922, aged 35.

At the foot of the church steps is a stretch of cobbled road marking the start of the Monte toboggan ride, and toboggan drivers hang about here, waiting for customers. The Jardim do Monte municipal garden is to the north of the steps, built around a short stretch of railway viaduct, now smothered in tropical greenery. The viaduct is a vestige of the rack-and-pinion railway that once linked Monte to Funchal. Having opened in 1894 to take tourists up and down, the railway was closed after an accident in 1939, when an engine blew up, killing four people.

In the opposite direction, it's a short walk to the **Monte Palace Tropical Garden,** laid out over 7ha (17 acres) of lush hillside. Here you can explore the garden's maze of paths leading to fishponds, grottoes and bridges, Japanese-style gates and gushing fountains. A short way back down the road to Funchal another garden has opened in the grounds of the **Quinta Jardins do Imperador,** where the Emperor Charles I lived out his brief exile.

✚ 138 D1 ✉ 6km (4 miles) north of Funchal 🍴 Cafés (€) on main square, and café/restaurant (€€) in Monte Palace Tropical Garden and in gardens of Quinta do Monte hotel (€) 🚠 Teleféricos da Madeiras, Teleféricos de Jardim Botânico or buses 20, 21, 22 ❓ Feast of the Assumption, 15 Aug

Monte Palace Tropical Garden
✉ Caminho do Monte 174 ☎ 782 339 🕐 Daily 9.30–6

Quinta Jardins do Imperador
✉ Caminho do Pico ☎ 780 460 🕐 Daily 10–6

PICO DO ARIEIRO
See pages 36–37.

PONTA DELGADA

The beachside church in Ponta Delgada contains the charred figure of the crucified Christ, which is taken in procession round the village during one of Madeira's biggest religious festivals, celebrated on the first Sunday in September. The miraculous figure was found washed up on the shore in the 16th century. In 1908 it survived a fire, which destroyed the rest of the church (now rebuilt and with a superb modern ceiling painting). Across from the church is a swimming pool complex with café.

The neighbouring village of Boaventura stands in a humid and fertile valley where willow plantations supply the raw material for the island's wicker industry (▶ 100–101). The palm-shaded cemetery shelters the grave of Miss Turner (died 1925), who never visited the spot in her lifetime but desired to be buried here because of her gardener's vivid accounts of the area's scenic beauty.

✚ 134 B1 ⊠ 51km (32 miles) north of Funchal 🍴 Solar de Boaventura (€€, ☎ 860 888), in Boaventura. Organic homegrown herbs, salads and vegetables 🚌 6

RIBEIRO FRIO

Ribeiro Frio is a delightful spot set among scented woodland. Here the fresh clean waters of the Ribeiro Frio ('cold river') are channelled into a series of deep pools to create a small trout farm. Trout inevitably feature on the menu of the restaurant alongside. Woodland glades on the opposite side of the road are planted with flowering trees and shrubs to create a miniature botanical garden, where basking butterflies add to the colour.

Ribeiro Frio is the meeting point of several *levada* walks. One of the easiest is the walk to Balcões, which you can pick up by walking downhill from the trout farm and taking the broad track to the left that leads to the *levada*. Follow the wide level path for about 10 minutes to reach Balcões, whose name means 'balcony'. The reason becomes obvious when you arrive: stunning landscapes open up from this hillside viewpoint across the sun-dappled Ametade Valley to the Penha de Águia (Eagle Rock), on Madeira's northern coast. The levada continues for another 2km (1.2 miles), with views of the bare volcanic peaks around Pico do Arieiro (➤ 36–37). On the opposite side of the road is Levada do Furado, signposted to Portela. If you walk as far as the bridge over the River Bezerro (allow an hour) you will experience a sequence of splendid views across central Madeira's mountainous green interior.

✚ 134 E4 ✉ 14km (8.5 miles) north of Funchal 🍴 Restaurante Ribeiro Frio (€€, ☎ 575 898), opposite the trout farm
🚌 56, 103, 138

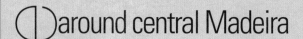

around central Madeira

This drive takes a whole day, encompassing fishing ports and wave-battered cliffs, green valleys and volcanic peaks.

Start early and head for Câmara de Lobos (➤ 84–85), hoping to catch the last of the bustle surrounding the town's fish market. Continue to Cabo Girão (➤ 24–25) for a dizzying peep over the top of Europe's second highest sea cliff.

At Ribeira Brava (➤ 77) you can enjoy a reviving cup of coffee in a seafront café before exploring the Manueline Church of São Bento.

Drive north up the terraced slopes of the valley of the Ribeira Brava to Boca da Encumeada (➤ 68–69) for views of the northern and southern coast of Madeira. Descend through woodland to São Vicente (➤ 80–81) and then follow the meandering north coast eastwards.

You may want to stop and swim at Ponta Delgada (➤ 90) before continuing on to Santana (➤ 94–97) for lunch or shopping, or to explore the theme park.

If you are feeling energetic, consider climbing Pico Ruivo (➤ 86–87). Alternatively, continue to Faial (➤ 85) and drive south to Ribeiro Frio (➤ 90–91) for a gentle stroll to Balcões. A third option is to continue on to the Poiso pass and drive west to the summit of Pico do Arieiro (➤ 36–37). From the Poiso pass the road descends via Terreiro da Luta (➤ 97) to Monte (➤ 88–89), where you can explore the Monte Palace Tropical Garden (open till 6, closed Sundays) before the short drive back to Funchal.

Distance 120km (75 miles)
Time 8 hours
Start/end point Funchal  Funchal 138 E1
Lunch O Virgílio (€) ✉ São Vicente ☎ 842 467

SANTANA

Santana's predominant colours are the greens of terraced fields
and hay meadows, interspersed by apple, pear and cherry

orchards. Dotted among the haystacks and the pollarded willows are triangular thatched buildings *(palheiros)*, used by local farmers as cow byres. Traditionally, people have lived in these ingenious structures too. Many are neglected and decaying, but a government scheme to encourage their restoration means that several in Santana are still inhabited. With their brightly painted triangular façades and a roof that sweeps from the ridge to the ground, these highly distinctive A-framed buildings are unique to this part of the island.

They are also surprisingly spacious, as you will discover if you visit the **Parque Temático da Madeira**, southwest of the town centre. As well as fully furnished houses, a corn mill and craft centre, the theme park has plenty of

play areas to keep energetic children amused and some excellent exhibits on the island's history and culture.

The EN 101-5 road south leads to Achada do Teixeira, from where you can walk to Pico Ruivo (➤ 86–87), Madeira's highest peak. Further north a rough minor road leads to the rest house at Queimadas. This marks the start of one of Madeira's finest *levada* walks, taking in spectacular ravines and primeval forest. The ultimate goal (reached after about an hour) is the 300m-high (985ft) waterfall that cascades into the pool at the bottom of the fern- and moss-filled Caldeirão Verde (Green Cauldron).

✚ 134 C4 ✉ Santana lies 42km (26 miles) north of Funchal 🍽 Several cafés and restaurants (€–€€) in the theme park; O Colmo (€€, ☎ 570 290) on the main street 🚌 56, 103, 132, 138

Parque Temático da Madeira

✉ Fonte da Pedra, just off main Santana to São Jorge road ☎ 570 410
🕐 Daily 10–7. Closed Mon mid-Sep to early Dec, mid-Jan to end Jun

TERREIRO DA LUTA

Terreiro da Luta consists of a massive monument to the Virgin, illuminated at night and visible from downtown Funchal. The monument was erected in 1927 in thanksgiving after German submarines, seeking to end the use of the island as a supply base, sank several ships and started shelling Funchal in 1916. The bombardment ceased after prayers to the Virgin. The massive chains surrounding the monument come from the anchors of the Allied ships sunk in the harbour.

A short way west of the monument is the neo-Gothic terminus of the Funchal to Monte railway, which closed in 1939 and has now been converted into the Au Gourmet de Quinta bar and restaurant. There are good views from the terrace, where you will find Francisco Franco's fine sculpture (dating from 1914) of Madeira's Portuguese discoverer, Captain Zarco.

✚ 138 D1 ✉ 8km (5 miles) north of Funchal 🍽 Au Gourmet de Quinta opposite (bar €, restaurant €€) 🚌 Buses 103, 138

Eastern Madeira

Although the landscapes of eastern Madeira are tamer than those of the central mountain range, they are not without their own drama, especially along the eastern spur where the island tails off in a sequence of wild cliffs and rocky islets dashed by the Atlantic waves. Inland there are lush green river valleys, some turned into manicured golf courses, others carved into tiny plots for growing fruit and vegetables.

The modern face of Madeira is represented by Santa Catarina and the free port at Caniçal, not to mention the tower blocks and holiday complexes of Madeira's second biggest town, Machico. A taste of Madeira's past survives at Caniçal, with its tuna-fishing fleet and Whaling Museum, and at Camacha, the centre of the island's wicker-weaving industry. As always on Madeira, the north coast is the place to go for solitude and a respite from modernity.

CAMACHA

The village of Camacha sits on a high plateau to the northeast of Funchal. To enjoy the panoramic views to be had from this elevated position, you have to visit the café called O Relógio (The Clock), on the main square. This former *quinta* (rural mansion) sports a squat clock tower, whose clock and bell were brought here from Liverpool in 1896 by the philanthropical Dr Michael Grabham. The eclectic and highly accomplished Grabham was an expert, among other things, on Madeiran flora, tropical fish, organs, clocks, volcanoes and electro-magnetism; once asked how he could speak with such erudition on so many subjects, he replied: 'What I do not know, I make up'.

In addition to the café and restaurant, **O Relógio** is the largest outlet on the island for Madeira's distinctive wicker products. Baskets and furniture fill every inch of available space – hanging from the ceilings as well as being piled on the floors – and nobody will pressurize you to buy as you explore the packed rooms.

Wicker is produced from the pollarded willows which thrive in the warm, humid valleys around Camacha. Cut back to a stunted and knobbly trunk each winter, the willows put out whip-like shoots, called osiers, up to 3m (10ft) in length. The osiers are placed in tanks and soaked in water until the bark is sufficiently pliable to be peeled from the core, then delivered to the cottages of wicker-workers, who boil the canes to make them supple before weaving them into everything from simple place mats and wastepaper baskets to peacock-backed chairs or ornate birdcages.

Demonstrations can sometimes be seen in the O Relógio basement, while the middle floor has a display of Noah's Ark animals and a galleon made by local weavers.

✚ 138 D3 ✉ 16km (10miles) northeast of Funchal 🚌 29, 77, 110

O Relógio

✉ Largo da Achada, Camacha ⏱ Open daily 9–6, except public hols
☎ 922 114 🍴 Café (€) on the ground floor of O Relógio

CANIÇAL

Caniçal was the centre of southern Europe's last whaling station until 1981, when the trade was banned by international treaty. Instrumental in the process of achieving the ban was the Society for the Protection of Marine Mammals, which helped establish the small but informative **Museu de Baleia** (Whaling Museum), now located in the offices once used by the Caniçal whaling company. Videos and displays in the museum explain how retired Madeiran fishermen have turned from whale-hunting to conservation, putting their knowledge of sperm whale habits and migration patterns at the disposal of marine biologists who have established a marine mammal sanctuary around Madeira.

To the east of the museum is a new port and working boatyard where fishing boats big and small, traditional and modern, are maintained and repaired. On the opposite side of the bay is a bathing complex and seafront restaurant.

✚ 139 B6 ✉ 32km (20 miles) east of Funchal 🍽 Cafés (€) next to museum and along the seafront 🚌 113

Museu de Baleia

✉ Largo da Lota ☎ 961 407 🕐 Tue–Sun 10–12, 1–6. Closed Mon ♿ Moderate

CANIÇO

Caniço is a sprawling village of two parts. The busy old town is set inland, its attractive buildings, the tree-shaded main square and 18th-century baroque church difficult to enjoy because of the traffic. Immediately south of the square, the pink-walled Quinta Splendida has a garden (open to the public during daylight hours) full of rare tropical varieties. To the south a winding road leads to a number of clifftop resort complexes, built here to take advantage of the sun and the sea views. Non-residents can pay to use the pool and sea-bathing facilities at the Roca Mar Hotel, and the clear waters here are popular with divers. A seafront promenade leads east to another pebbly bathing spot at Praia dos Reis Magos.

✚ 138 E3 ✉ 8km (5 miles) east of Funchal Elsidro café (€€, ☎ 934 342) next to the church 🚌 2, 109, 110, 155

GARAJAU

Garajau is Portuguese for 'tern', and the village is named after the attractive black-headed sea birds that nest on the nearby cliffs. You may catch sight of them hovering over the limpid blue sea before plunging into the water to catch their food.

Garajau's most prominent landmark is the huge statue of Christ, erected in 1927. Similar to the larger and more famous statues in Lisbon and Rio de Janeiro, it stands with outstretched arms on a headland 200m (656ft) above the sea. From here you can walk down a cobbled track leading to the base of the cliffs, where a concrete causeway links several boulder-strewn coves and beaches.

✚ 138 E3 ✉ 8km (5 miles) east of Funchal 🍴 Snack Bar O Neptuno at the lower end of Garajau's main street, on the opposite side of the road to the Dom Pedro Hotel 🚌 2, 109, 110, 155

MACHICO

Machico is where Zarco first set foot on Madeira in 1420, claiming for Portugal an island that had been known to sailors for thousands of years. Among those who got to Madeira before Zarco were Robert Machin and Anne of Hereford, shipwrecked here after their storm-tossed ship was driven out into the Atlantic from the coast of Portugal. Robert and Anne died within days of each other and were buried by the rest of the crew, who later escaped by building a raft. On finding their graves some 50 years later, Zarco is said to have named the spot Machico, in Machin's honour (in fact, it is more likely that Machico is a corruption of Monchique, Zarco's home town in Portugal).

Zarco and his fellow navigator, Tristão Vaz Teixeira, were appointed governors of Madeira in 1425, with Zarco ruling the west from Funchal, and Teixeira in charge of the east, based in

Machico. It is his statue that stands in front of the town's large 15th-century parish church.

The smaller Capela dos Milagres (Chapel of the Miracles), east of the town, is reputed to be built on the site of Machin's grave. The original church was washed away by flash floods in 1803, but the beautiful Gothic crucifix from the high altar was found floating at sea and returned by an American sailor.

Machico's third church (under restoration) was built in 1739. It stands on the western arm of Machico's wide bay, where the triangular fortress, built in 1706, now serves as the tourist office. This toy-town fort is partnered by the Fórum Machico, a cultural centre housing a library, cinema and theatre, plus a first-floor café with sweeping views over the town's wide bay.

✚ 139 C5 ✉ 24km (15 miles) northeast of Funchal 🍽 Cafés and restaurants in Rua do Mercado (Market Street), including Mercado Velho (Rua do Mercado €€, ☎ 965 926) 🚌 20, 23, 53, 78, 113, 156 ❓ Festa di Santissimo Sacramento (Feast of the Holy Sacrament), celebrated on the last weekend in Aug; procession in honour of Nosso Senhora de Milagres (Our Lord of Miracles) 8–9 October 🛈 Forte de Nossa Senhora do Amparo (☎ 962 289 🕐 Mon–Fri 9–12.30, 2–5, Sat 9.30–12)

to Ponta de São Lourenço

Follow this switchback path to the easternmost tip of Madeira and you will feel as if you are standing on the edge of the world.

To reach the start of the walk, drive east along the EN 101-3 through Caniçal (▶ 102–103) and past Prainha beach (▶ 109), until you come to a small roundabout. The left turn leads to a well-placed miradouro with panoramic views. Take the right turn and continue to the car park at the end of the tarmac road. The path starts by the big boulders at the eastern end of the car park. So many people now use the path it is well worn and impossible to miss.

To your right is the great rocky sweep of the Baía de Abra (Abra Bay), with its towering orange and brown cliffs. Beyond the bay is Ilhéu de Fora, with its lighthouse, and an eyelet in the rock called Ponta do Furado. Further out to sea are the flat-topped Ilhas Desertas, inhabited only by seabirds and a small colony of protected monk seals.

After 20 minutes or so, the uphill track meets a boulder wall, with a gap for walkers to pass through. Bear left on a rocky path and descend to the valley where the path splits.

Go left to reach a viewpoint high above three purple rocks known as the 'seahorses', with a stunning westwards view of high cliffs and raging seas.

Brave souls with a good head for heights can continue from here along the waymarked path for another 1.5km (1 mile) to the little quay called the Cais do Sardinha, a now deserted harbour named after its former owners, but for most visitors the first viewpoint will be excitement enough.

Distance 2km (1.2 miles)
Time 1.5 hours
Start/end point Car park at easternmost end of EN 101-3 road, beyond Caniçal ✚ 139 B6
Lunch No café nearby but stallholders occasionally turn up in the car park to sell fruit and cold drinks

PALHEIRO GARDENS

See pages 34–35.

PORTO DA CRUZ

Porto da Cruz was once an important harbour town on the north coast of Madeira, thriving in an era when goods were transported from place to place by boat, but declining into a quiet backwater once road transport took over. Today it is a town in transition, its old fishing quarter, threaded by cobbled alleys, partly restored and partly still crumbling.

The old port is reached by following the road that skirts the small fortress-crowned hill to the east. Continuing round the hill, you will reach the sugar mill and distillery of the Companhia dos Enghenos do Norte. The mill stands unused for much of the year, but a sweet scent fills the air during the sugar harvesting – March to May – when production of *aguardente*, a rum-like spirit, is under way.

Something of the gloom that visitors to Porto da Cruz claim to experience is due to the shadows cast by Penha de Águia (Eagle Rock), rising to a height of 590m (1,935ft) to the west of the village. The road to the east of the village gives out at Lorano, and from here there are splendid views to be had from the clifftop path.
➕ 138 A3 ✉ 30km (18 miles) northeast of Funchal 🍴 Praça do Engeno restaurant (€€), Rua da Praia 🚌 53, 56, 78, 103, 138

PRAINHA

Prainha enjoys the unique distinction of having the largest natural sand beach on Madeira. Hidden from the road, the beach is reached from the car park on the road from Caniçal to Ponta de São Lourenço.

The size of the car park indicates how busy the beach can become in summer. The brown-black sand on the beach derives from the local rock, a curious mixture of crushed shell and volcanic debris, pulverized by tens of thousands of years of wave action. The sheltered, south-facing beach enjoys good views of the easternmost tip of Madeira, as well as of aeroplanes flying into nearby Santa Catarina airport.

➕ 139 B6 ✉ 30km (18 miles) east of Funchal 🍴 Bar (€), overlooking the beach 🚌 113

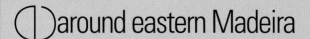

around eastern Madeira

Allow at least half a day for this leisurely drive around Madeira's eastern spur, including time to swim off one of the island's few naturally sandy beaches.

Leave Funchal on the ER 101, following signs to the airport, then turn left, after 3km (2 miles), on to the ER 102 signposted to Camacha.

After 2km (1.2 miles) turn right to visit the Blandy wine-merchant family's splendid Palheiro Gardens (➤ 34–35).

Rejoin the ER 102 and continue north to Camacha (➤ 100–101). Continue along the ER 102 for a further 11km (7 miles) to Santo António da Serra.

At Santo António da Serra take a stroll in the park surrounding the Quinta da Serra (➤ 115), the home of the Blandy family before they acquired the Quinta do Palheiro Ferreiro.

Continue along the ER 101 but turn left, before reaching Machico, on the ER 101-3 signposted to Caniçal. Skirt Caniçal and continue to the end of the road for a walk out across the cliff tops at Ponta de São Lourenço (➤ 106–107).

Cool off from your walk by taking a dip in the sea at Prainha beach (➤ 109) on the way back to Caniçal, with its Whaling Museum (➤ 102). Stop at Machico (➤ 104), Madeira's second town, to walk around the bay and visit the three historic churches.

Follow the coastal road beneath the airport runway to Santa Cruz (► 112–113).

Depending on the time of day, your last stop before returning to Funchal could be Garajau (► 104), where you can watch the sun go down from the clifftop alongside the outsize statue of Christ.

Distance 60km (37 miles)
Time 6 hours
Start/end point Funchal ⊠ 138 E1
Lunch Café O Relógio (€€) ⊠ Largo da Achada, Camacha
☎ 922 114

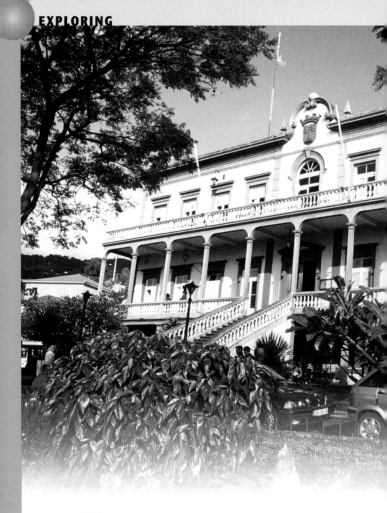

SANTA CRUZ

Despite the proximity of Santa Catarina airport, which opened
in 1964, Santa Cruz manages to retain the peaceful atmosphere
of a bygone era. The parish church of 1479 is one of the oldest on
the island and echoes of Funchal's cathedral suggest that the
same architect – Pedro Enes – could have been involved in the

design. Three blocks east of the main square, in Rua da Ponta Nova, is the 19th-century Tribunal (Law Court). Flowering trees fill the park surrounding the court, while date palms and dragon trees line the seafront road, two blocks south, lending the pebble beach the air of an upmarket Riviera.

Strung out along the promenade are cafés, the village market, the Municipal Library with a small art gallery and an open-air theatre, plus the Palm Beach lido, with paddling pools and a swimming pool.

Aquaparque, a water park at the other (western) end of the town, has slides, tubes and flumes, and is a great place for children to let off steam.

🚹 138 D4 ⊠ 17km (10.5 miles) east of Funchal 🍽 Cafés along the seafront (€) serving homemade cakes 🚌 20, 23, 53, 113, 128, 156

Aquaparque
⊠ Ribeira do Boaventura (just west of Santa Cruz) ☎ 324 412 🕐 Daily 10–7 (to 7.30 in summer)

SANTO ANTÓNIO DA SERRA

The wooded slopes around Santo António da Serra (known locally as just Santo da Serra) are dotted with the elegant old mansions of the English merchants who once dominated the Madeira wine trade. Privacy, and a welcome climate several degrees cooler than downtown Funchal, made this a favoured summer retreat.

One splendid mansion, the Quinta da Serra, stands at the centre of a large public park, just off the main square, where there are a few animal enclosures and a playground. The park is at its most colourful during the spring and early summer when the first flush of camellias is superseded by the bright blooms of azaleas. Avenues running through the park lead to a viewpoint that looks out to the easternmost tip of the island.

✚ 138 C4 ✉ 22km (13.5 miles) northeast of Funchal 🍴 Café (€) on the main square 🚌 Buses 20, 77, 78 ❓ Park open daily during daylight hours

Porto Santo

Porto Santo is all about sun, sea and sand, and almost nothing else. The sleepy island is virtually flat, and there is little agriculture since Porto Santo lacks Madeira's abundant supplies of water. The island's population of 5,000 earns much of its living during July and August, when a steady stream of visitors arrives to soak up the sun and dance the night away in hotel discos.

Some take the relatively expensive 15-minute flight from Madeira, while others take a more leisurely sea journey on the Porto Santo Line's luxurious cruiser, which takes 2 hours and 40 minutes to cross the 37km (23 miles) of choppy ocean separating the two islands. Plans are afoot to develop Porto Santo's tourism further, but for now its chief attraction is that its magnificent sweep of beach remains clean, unspoiled and undeveloped.

FONTE DA AREIA

The little rain that Porto Santo receives rapidly filters through the island's sandy soils to emerge as a series of springs when the water meets impermeable basalt. The Fonte da Areia (Spring in the Sand) is one such spring, and its popularity is guaranteed by the belief that drinking its waters restores body and soul and bestows longevity. For those who prefer alternative restoratives, there is a bar alongside the public drinking fountain, with palm-shaded tables creating a tropical illusion. The spring itself fills a series of troughs that were once used by local women for washing their laundry. The nearby cliffs of compressed sand have been eroded into bizarre sculptures by wind and rain, and there are rock pools to explore on the pebbly beach below. The spring can be reached on foot by taking the road west from Camacha; the Fonte da Areia makes a good destination for a day trip and, perhaps, a picnic.

✚ 140 B4 ✉ 3km (2 miles) northwest of Vila Baleira 🍴 Café (€) alongside the spring

PONTA DA CALHETA

This southernmost tip of Porto Santo marks the watershed between the long sweep of sandy beach running along the southern coast of the island and the rocky northern coast. A good time to come here is dusk, when the setting sun casts shadows and colours over the much-eroded rocks on the offshore islands, allowing you to exercise your imagination and see all sorts of shapes. The evening can be extended by taking a meal of fresh fish in the nearby restaurant, then walking back along the sandy beach while imagining you are in your own private paradise.

✚ 140 E3 ✉ 5km (3 miles) southwest of Vila Baleira 🍴 O Calhetas restaurant (€€, ☎ 984 380) at the point where the coastal road ends

PORTELA

The *miradouro* (viewpoint) at Portela may not be the highest point
on Porto Santo, but it is the best place to get a sense of the scale
of the pure sandy beach that seems to stretch endlessly along the
southern coast. It will also give you an idea of why Porto Santo is
known as the 'tawny island'. Deforestation at a very early stage in
the island's history led to rapid erosion of the fertile topsoil, leaving
the sand-coloured landscape you see today.

✚ 141 C6 ✉ 1.5km (1 mile) northeast of Vila Baleira

SERRA DO DENTRO

The landscape of the Serra do Dentro Valley, forming the eastern part of the island, looks like the setting for a Wild West movie with its arid sheep- and cattle-grazed slopes. The terraces, abandoned farmhouses and threshing floors are all that remain of communities that gave up the struggle to scratch a living from the thin soil, while reservoirs and stunted tree saplings indicate government schemes to restore life to the area.

✚ 141 B6 ✉ 5km (3 miles) northeast of Vila Baleira

through the quarries and coves of Porto Santo

Geological formations and beautiful coves are found at the unspoiled southwestern tip of Porto Santo. Heading for Calheta by bus, taxi, car or bicycle, you pass the turning for Campo de Baixo, with its church of Espírito Santo (Holy Spirit) and look for the next turn right. If you come by car you can park here.

Walk up the track, turning left after 50m (55yds), and continue to the little white chapel of São Pedro (St Peter), originally built in the 17th century.

As you continue straight on, climbing the low conical hill called the Pico de Ana Ferreira (283m/928ft), you will reach a redundant quarry remarkable for its much-photographed basalt columns, popularly known as 'organ pipes', that are formed by the slow cooling of volcanic magma.

Return the way you came to the main coast road and continue towards Calheta. After 2.5km (1.5 miles), take another right turn and after 0.75km (0.4 miles) look for a path on the left that climbs then descends for 0.75km (0.4 miles).

At the end of the descent you will reach the tiny beach and clear turquoise waters of the cove at Zimbralinho (shaded from mid afternoon, so aim to get here by the middle of the day if you want the best sunshine).

Retracing your steps, continue west until the road runs out at Ponta da Calheta.

The café here is a good spot to enjoy a long lazy lunch with views that, on a clear day, stretch to Madeira. Afterwards you can swim before taking the bus back to Vila Baleira (last departure 6.20pm).

Distance 5.5km (3.5 miles) on foot
Time 3 hours
Start point Vila Baleira ✚ 141 C5
End point Ponta da Calheta ✚ 140 E3
Lunch O Calhetas (€€€, ☎ 984 380), Ponta da Calheta beach

VILA BALEIRA

Vila Baleira is Porto Santo's capital, and it is here that most of the island's 5,000 inhabitants live. The town was founded by Bartolomeu Perestrelo, the first governor, who did not draw the short straw you might think from the island's present appearance: in the 15th century it was a profitable colony, producing cereals, wines and sugar, as well as dyestuffs from the sap of dragon trees.

Two dragon trees survive in the town's main square, Largo do Pelourinho, flanking the entrance to the 16th-century Town Hall, with its handsome double staircase and 16th-century stone doorframe. Alongside is the popular Bar Gel Burger, the centre of the island's social life. To the north is the much-restored parish church, with only a small side chapel surviving from the 15th-century Gothic original. From opposite the Town Hall, Rua Infante D Henrique, the town's palm-lined main street, leads straight to the beach, the objective of most visitors.

In the street behind the church is the **Casa Museu Cristóvão Colombo,** reputed to be the house in which Christopher Columbus lived during his stay on Porto Santo. There is a good library of books in English, Portuguese and other languages, from which you can learn all there is to know about the famous Genoese explorer, and several imaginative portraits and amusing prints depict the arrival of some of the first Europeans to land on American shores.

✚ 141 C5 ✉ On the southern coast of Porto Santo, 10 minutes' drive from the airport 🍴 The Baiana café (€, ☎ 984 649), on Largo do Pelourinho, serves excellent grilled fish

ℹ Rua Dr Henrique Vieira de Castro (☎ 982 361)

Casa Museu Cristóvão Colombo

☎ 952 598 🕐 Tue–Fri 10–12.30, 2–5.30, Sat 10–1 (Jul–Sep only). Closed Sun, public hols

a drive

around Porto Santo

Take a taxi, or rent a car, for a half-day tour of Porto Santo's main sights.

From Vila Baleira follow Rua Bispo D E de Alencastre eastwards (signposted to Serra de Fora).

The road takes you to the viewpoint at Portela (➤ 120) and on to the farming villages of Serra da Fora and Serra do Dentro (➤ 121). The views change as you swing round the north side of the island to Camacha, with its restored windmill and the Estrela do Norte restaurant, which is housed in an old farmhouse and specializes in barbecued chicken.

In Camacha, take the minor road that leads to the Fonte da Areia to sample the waters, which are reputed to bestow eternal youth on those who drink them. Return to the main road and drive south for 2km (1 mile), then turn left on the minor road that goes to the viewpoint on Pico do Castelo (437m/1,434ft).

From the cone-shaped peak there are sweeping views over the whole island, with the airport runway prominent in the plain to the west. On the summit you will find the scant remains of the fortification after which the Pico do Castelo is named. Islanders used to take refuge on those frequent occasions when pirates raided Vila Baleira. Warning bonfires were lit on the neighbouring hill, called Pico do Facho (Beacon Peak), the island's highest point at 517m (1,696ft).

You can walk from one peak to the other through pine plantations before heading back downhill for the short return stretch to Vila Baleira.

Distance 15km (10 miles)
Time 3 hours
Start/end point Vila Baleira ✚ 141 C5
Lunch Estrela do Norte (€, ☎ 983 500), a busy bar in Camacha, with an open-air terrace serving inexpensive charcoal-grilled fish and chicken

Index

Acknowledgements

The Automobile Association would like to thank the following photographers, companies and picture libraries for their assistance in the preparation of this book.

Abbreviations for the picture credits are as follows – (t) top; (b) bottom; (c) centre; (l) left; (r) right; (AA) AA World Travel Library.

4l Airport, AA/P Baker; **4c** Pico do Arieiro, AA/C Sawyer; **4r** Former Monte Palace Hotel, AA/J Wyand; **5l** Palheiro Gardens, AA/C Sawyer; **5c** Palacio de Sol, AA/P Baker; **6/7** Airport, AA/P Baker; **10** Child at Flower Festival, Funchal, AA/C Sawyer; **12** Airport, AA/P Baker; **13** Ponta do Sol, AA/P Baker; **15** Boat from Cani, AA/J Wyand; **16** Bank of Madeira, Funchal, AA/J Wyand; **18** Policeman, AA/P Baker; **20/21** Pico do Arieiro, AA/C Sawyer; **22** Adegas de Sao Francisco, AA/C Sawyer; **22/23** Adegas de Sao Francisco, AA/P Baker; **23** Adegas de Sao Francisco, AA/C Sawyer; **24/25** Cabo Girao, AA/C Sawyer; **26/27** Curral das Freiras, AA/C Sawyer; **27** Curral das Freiras, AA/C Sawyer; **28** Mercado dos Lavradores in Funchal, AA/J Wyand; **29** Mercado dos Lavradores in Funchal, AA/P Baker; **30/31** Monte Taboggan Ride, AA/J Wyand; **31** Tiles depicting Monte Taboggan Ride, AA/C Sawyer; **32** Museu de Arte Sacra, Funchal, AA/J Wyand; **32/33** Museu de Arte Sacra, Funchal, AA/J Wyand; **34** Palheiro Gardens, AA/C Sawyer; **34/35** Palheiro Gardens topiary, AA/C Sawyer; **35** Palheiro Gardens, AA/C Sawyer; **36/37** Pico do Arieiro, AA/C Sawyer; **38** Se (Funchal Cathedral) AA/C Sawyer; **38/39** Se (Funchal Cathedral) AA/C Sawyer; **40** Zona Velha (Old Town), Funchal, AA/C Sawyer; **40/41** Zona Velha (Old Town), Funchal, AA/J Wyand; **42/43** Former Monte Palace Hotel, AA/J Wyand; **45** Funchal street, AA/C Sawyer; **47** Convento de Santa Clara, AA/C Sawyer; **48** Fortaleza de Sao Tiago, AA/C Sawyer; **48/49** IBTAM Handicrafts Institute, AA/C Sawyer; **50/51** Jardim Botanico, AA/J Wyand; **51** Jardim dos Loiros, AA/J Wyand; **52/53** Jardim de Santa Catarina, AA/J Wyand; **54** Tiles at the Museu 'A Cidade do Acucar, AA/J Wyand; **56/57** Museu Franco, AA/J Wyand; **58** Painting at the Museu Freitas, AA/J Wyand; **58/59** Museu Municipal, AA/J Wyand; **60** Praca do Municipio, AA/C Sawyer; **62** O Patio AA/C Sawyer; **63** Funchal, AA/J Wyand; **65** Quinta das Cruzes, AA/C Sawyer; **66** Flower Festival, AA/C Sawyer; **67** North Coast Drive, AA/C Sawyer; **68/69** Boca da Encumeada, AA/C Sawyer; **69** Calheta, AA/J Wyand; **70** Ponta do Pargo lighthouse, AA/J Wyand; **71** Paul da Serra, AA/J Wyand; **72/73t** Ponta do Sol, AA/C Sawyer; **72/73b** Porto Moniz, Roberto Pereira; **75** Levada do Risco, AA/C Sawyer; **76/77** Ribeira Brava, AA/P Baker; **79** North Coast Drive, AA/C Sawyer; **80/81** Sao Vicente, AA/C Sawyer; **82** North Coast Drive, AA/C Sawyer; **83** Pico Ruivo, AA/J Wyand; **84/85** Camara de Lobos, AA/J Wyand; **87** Pico Ruivo, AA/J Wyand; **88** Taboggan run, Monte, AA/C Sawyer; **88/89** Monte Palace Tropical Garden, AA/C Sawyer; **90** Ponta Delgada, AA/J Wyand; **90/91** Ribeiro Frio, AA/J Wyand; **91** Lady knitting at Ribeiro Frio, AA/C Sawyer; **93** Cabo Girão, AA/J Wyand; **94/95** Santana, AA/C Sawyer; **96** Terreiro da Luta, AA/C Sawyer; **98** Madeira Wine Company barrel, AA/J Wyand; **99** Boat at Canical AA/C Sawyer; **100t** Wicker animals at Camacha, AA/P Baker; **100b** Willow trees at Camacha, AA/P Baker; **100/101** Willow weavers, AA/C Sawyer; **102t** Souvenirs at Caniçal, AA/P Baker; **102/103** Beached boat at Caniçal, AA/C Sawyer; **103** Caniço, AA/J Wyand; **104** Garajau, AA/J Wyand; **104/105** Machico, AA/C Sawyer; **106/107** Ponta de São Lourenco, AA/C Sawyer; **108/109** Porto da Cruz, AA/J Wyand; **111** Machico, AA/C Sawyer; **112/113** Santa Cruz, AA/P Baker; **114** Santo António da Serra, AA/P Baker; **115** Santo António da Serra, AA/P Baker; **116** Boat in Câmara de Lobos harbour, AA/C Sawyer; **117** Porto Santo harbour, AA/J Wyand; **118** Fonte da Areia in Porto Santo, DRTM; **118/119** Calheta in Porto Santo, Marcial Fernandes; **120/121** Portela, AA/J Wyand; **123** Passeios in Porto Santo, Marcial Fernandes; **124** Porto Santo AA/J Wyand; **126** Porto Santo, AA/J Wyand.

Every effort has been made to trace the copyright holders, and we apologise in advance for any accidental errors. We would be happy to apply the corrections in the following edition of this publication.

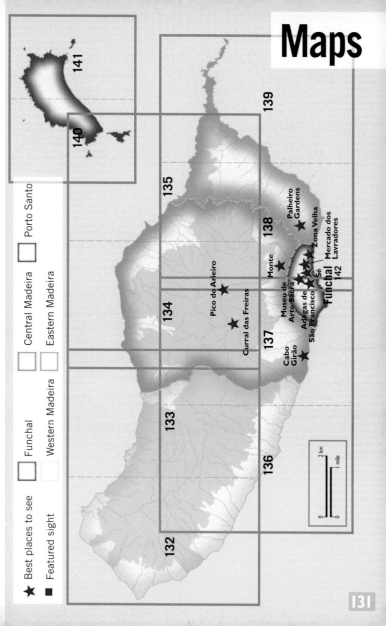

Maps

Best places to see ★

Featured sight ■

Funchal

Central Madeira

Porto Santo

Western Madeira

Eastern Madeira

141

140

139

135

138

Palheiro Gardens ★

Zona Velha

Mercado dos Lavradores

134

Pico do Arieiro ★

Monte ★

Sé

Funchal

142

137

Curral das Freiras ★

Museu de Arte Sacra ★

Adegas de São Francisco ★

Cabo Girão ★

133

136

132

2 km
1 mile
0

131

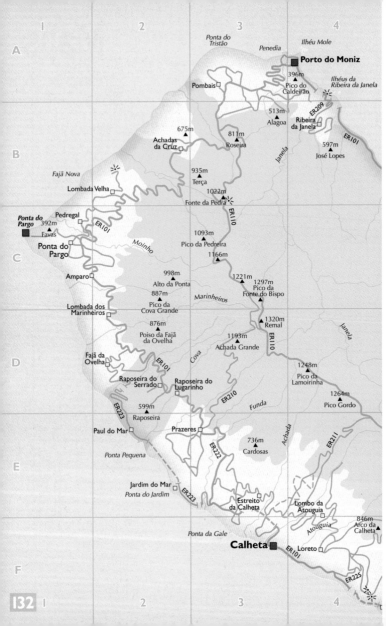

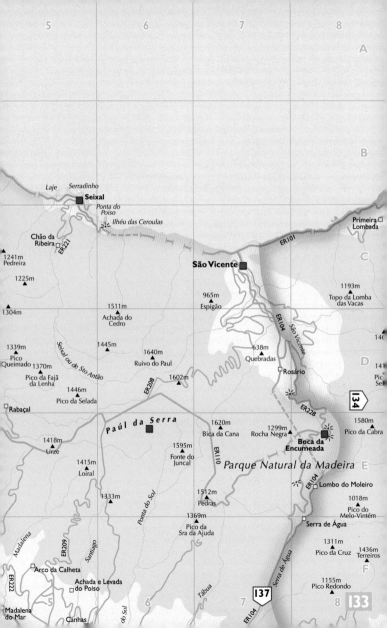

1

2

3

4

Ponta de São Jorge

Pontinha
Caes

Ponta Delgada

Pontinha

Arco de
São Jorge

São Jorge

507m
Rainha

Achada da Cruz

ER101

Boaventura

825m

Ribeira
Funda

346m
Pinheiro

Primeira
Lombada

Arco de
São Jorge

Pordão

São Jorge

Ilha

Santana

1094m
Estreitinho

Lombo do Meio

Bonita

ER218

1193m
opo da Lomba
das Vacas

ER107

1184m
Assumadouros

981m
Vale da Lara

864m
Redondo

1468m

Achada da
Madeira

1326m
Pico das
Lajinhas

1302m
Pico das Pédras

1418m
Pico da
Selada

1592m
Canario

1592m
Achada do
Teixeira

1407m
Chiceiros da
Queimada

Urzal

1410m
Pico da
Escada

1649m
Pico das
Eirinhas

1861m
Pico Ruivo
de Santana

Seca

1580m
Pico da Cabra

1725m
Casado

1455m
Pico das
Empenas

1851m
Pico das Torres

bo do Moleiro

1654m
Pico do
Grande

1170m
Pico da
Nogueira

Ribeiro Frio

1018m
Pico do
Melo-Vintém

★ 1818m

1476m

ER103

1177m

Água

1443m

Pico do Arieiro

1759m
Cedro

1699m ER202
ER202

Cabeço da
Lenha

Poço do Be

1m
a Cruz

1436m
Terreiros

★ Curral das
Freiras

1492m

ER215

ER2

1235m
ndo

1088m
Pico do
Serrado

1481m
Chão dos
Balcões

1413m

Porto

Pico da
Malhada

137

1344m
Esteios

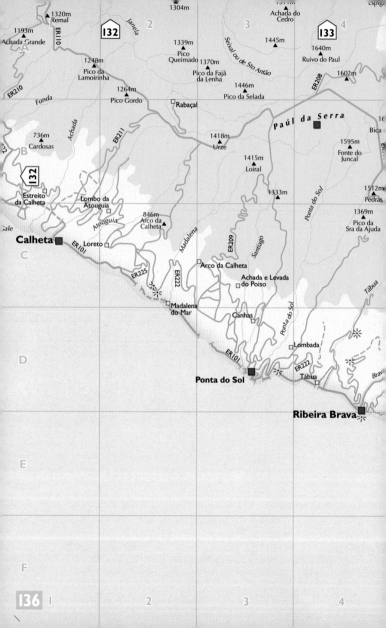

1304m

1320m
Remal

Achada do
Cedro

Espiga

1193m
Achada Grande

ER110

132

1445m

133

1339m
Pico
Queimado

1248m
Pico da
Lamoirinha

1370m
Pico da Fajã
da Lenha

1640m
Ruivo do Paul

ER208

1602m

Janela

Sesal ou de Sto Antão

ER210

Funda

1264m
Pico Gordo

Rabaçal

1446m
Pico da Selada

Paúl da Serra

Bica

Achada

ER211

736m
Cardosas

B

1418m
Urze

1595m
Fonte do
Juncal

132

1415m
Loiral

1512m
Pedras

Estreito
da Calheta

Lombo da
Atouguia

1333m

Ponta do Sol

1369m
Pico da
Sra da Ajuda

846m
Arco da
Calheta

Atouguia

Madalena

ER209

Santiago

Gale

Calheta

ER101
Loreto

C

Arco da Calheta

Tábua

ER225

ER222

Achada e Levada
do Poiso

Madalena
do Mar

Canhas

Ponta do Sol

D

ER101

Lombada

ER222

Ponta do Sol

Tábua

Brava

Ribeira Brava

E

F

1

2

3

4

das Vacas

638m
Quebradas

Rosário

São Vicente

ER104

ER228

1299m
Rocha Negra

Cana

0m

Parque Natural da Madeira

Boca da
Encumeada

ER104

Lombo do Moleiro

1580m
Pico da Cabra

Serra de Água

1311m
Pico da Cruz

1436m
Terreiros

1155m
Pico Redondo

Serra de Água

ER104

Campanário

Lugar da
Serra

786m
Pico da Coroa

ER229

Pedra de
Nossa Senhora

Campanário

Quinta Grande

R101

631m
Galo

Cabo Girão

Câmara de
Lobos

ER229

1468m
Achada da
Madeira

1418m
Pico da
Selada

1410m
Pico da
Escada

Urzal

1725m
Casado

1455m
Pico das
Empenas

1654m
Pico do
Grande

1018m
Pico do
Melo-Vintém

1443m

1235m
Pico da
Malhada

956m
Cruz das Mocas

Estreito de
Câmara de Lobos

ER229

1184m
Assumadouros

1326m
Pico das
Lajinhas

1592m
Canario

1649m
Pico das
Eirinhas

Curral das
Freiras

1088m
Pico do
Serrado

ER107

Socorridos

981m
Vale da Lara

134

1592m
Achada do
Teixeira

1861m
Pico Ruivo
de Santana

1851m
Pico das Torres

1818m
Pico do Arieiro

1759m
Cedro

1699m ER202

138

1344m
Esteios

Santa Luzia

Bonita

Pi

São João

São Roque

Santo António

ER106

São Martinho

R101

Forte de
Pico

261m
Ponta da Cruz

Ponta Gorda

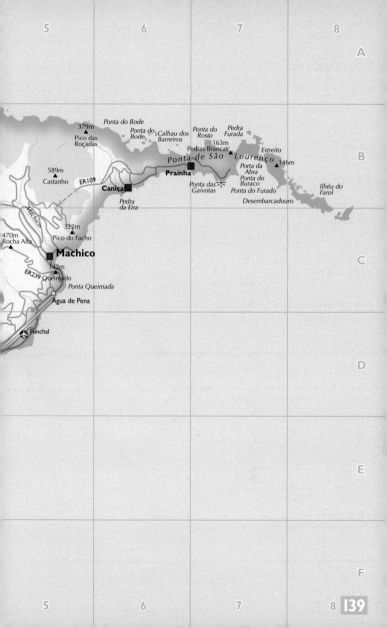

Ilhéu da Fonte
da Areia

Rocha do Gasparão

Fonte da Areia   125m ▲
Farrobo

Ponta do Varadouro

Urnal Grande   227m ▲
                            Barbara
                            Gomes   138m ▲

Tabaqueira   176m ▲   Cochino

                                             Campo de Cima

São Sebastião   Salgado   Lomb

                                  Campo de Baixo

Ponta de Oeste   Ponta da Canaveira   283m ▲
                                    270m ▲ Pico de
Ilhéu de Ferro   115m ▲   Espigão Ana Ferreira

Ponta de Cabra   117m ▲   Ponta
                    Focinho do Urso
Ponta do Gabriel   184m ▲

                    Ponta da Calheta

Boqueirão de Baixo
Pedra Branca

              179m ▲

Moledo Ruivo
                        Portinho
              Ilhéu de Baixo ou da Cal

Ponta da Isabel   167m ▲

Ponta do
Patacho
Ponta do Ilhéu

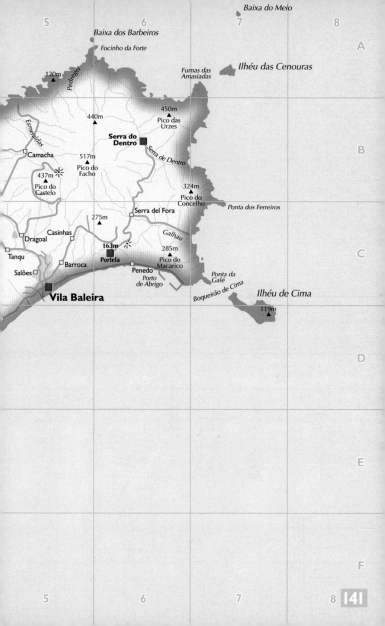

5   6   7   8

A

Baixa dos Barbeiros

Focinho da Forte

Ilhéu das Cenouras

120m

Pedregal

Furnas das Amasiadas

450m
▲
Pico das Urzes

440m
▲

Espmeraldas

Serra do Dentro

Serra de Dentro

B

☐ Camacha

517m
▲
Pico do Facho

437m ☼
▲
Pico do Castelo

324m
▲
Pico do Concelho

Ponta dos Ferreiros

Serra del Fora

275m
▲

Galhau

☐ Casinhas

163m ☼
■
Portela

285m
▲
Pico do Macarico

C

☐ Dragoal

☐

☐ Tanqu

☐ Barroca

Penedo ☐

Porto de Abrigo

Ponta da Galé

Salões ☐

Boqueirão de Cima

Ilhéu de Cima

Vila Baleira

119m
▲

D

E

F

Funchal

142

Parque de Santa Catarina

Fortaleza do Pico

Convento de Santa Clara

Quinta das Cruzes

Museu Freitas

Museu Municipal

Biblioteca Inglesa

Igreja Inglesa

Igreja de Santa Catarina

AVENIDA SA CARNEIRO

Estrada da Pontinha

Praça do Infante

RUA DA FONTE

AVENIDA ARRIAGA

AVENIDA DO MAR

AVENIDA DO MAR

Cais

Jardim de São Francisco

Igreja de São Francisco

Igreja Escocesa

Rua Ivens

Rua São Francisco

Rua da Carreira

São Pedro Igreja

Igreja de São Pedro

Rua do Seminário

Rua da Mouraria

Calçada de Santa Clara

Cruz Vermelha

Rua das Mercês

Rua dos Ferreiros

Rua dos Netos

CTAB

Instituto do Vinho e Museu

Rua 31 de Janeiro

Rua 5 de Outubro

Adegas de São Francisco

Palacio de S. Lourenço

Palácio de São Pedro Regional

Pátio

CTA

Avenida Zarco

Rua do Bispo

Rua da Alfandega

Rua dos Murças

Rua da Sé

RUA ALUBE

Museu de Arte Sacra

SÉ

A Cidade do Açúcar

Museu de "A Cidade do Açúcar"

Igreja do Colégio

Praça do Município

Tribunal e Câmara

Igreja do Carmo

Rua do Carmo

Rua da Carreira

Rua das Pretas

Rua dos Aranhas

Rua do Castanheiro

R. C. Pestana

Rua da Queimada de Cima

Rua da Queimada de Baixo

Rua dos Ferreiros

R M Funchal

Santa Luzia

Rua de Santa Maria

Rua da Conceição

Rua de Santa Luzia

Parliament e Museu

Praça do Colombo

Rua do Sabão

Rua da Alfandega

Rua de Esmeralda

Praça da Praia

Edifício da Alfandega

AVENIDA DO MAR

AVENIDA DO MAR

Praça de Autonomia

Praça de São Tiago

Rua 5 de Outubro

Rua dos Tanoeiros

Rua Direita

RUA DE FERNÃO ORNELAS

Rua do Seminário

Rua da Fábrica

Rua das Hortas

Igreja do Bom Jesus

Igreja do Carmo

RUA DO BOM JESUS

Rua de Bela

Rua do Ribeirinho d Baixo

Rua d Hospital Velho

DO VISCONDE DO ANADIA

RUA BRIGADEIRO OUDINOT

Mercado dos Lavradores

Madeira Story Centre

João Gomes

Rua Profeta

Rua de Santa Maria

Rua Boa Viagem

Rua Latino Coelho

Rua da Infância

Rua Ornelas

Rua da Infância

RUA BRIGADEIRO OUDINOT

Escola Secundária Francisco Franco

Museu Franco

RUA DE JOÃO DE DEUS

J. Convenience

IBTAM Handicrafts Institute

R DR MANUEL PESTANA JUNIOR

Rua de Don Carlos

Rua Conselheiro A Pestana

Rua Bela São Tiago

Clube de Jazz da Madeira

Igreja de São Tiago

Corpo Santo

Tenis

Tennis

Campo do Liceu

RUA NOVA DE ALEGRIA

RUA DO CONDE DO CARVALHAL

RUA NOVA DE ALEGRIA

Jardim Botânico; Jardim dos Loiros

Rua da Rochinha

Zona Velha

Fortaleza de São Tiago

0 200 m
0 200 yds